29

"EAMON DE VALERA
1882—1975"

THE CONTROVERSIAL GIANT
OF MODERN IRELAND

*A survey in text and pictures of the
life and influence of a famous leader*

PUBLISHED BY THE IRISH TIMES, LIMITED

© 1976 The Irish Times Limited
13 D'Olier Street, Dublin 2, Republic of Ireland

Editor and Designer: Peter Tynan O'Mahony
Photographic sources: The Irish Times · Irish Press Group
J. Cashman · National Library of Ireland
Aras de Valera Museum · Charles C. Fennell
National Gallery of Ireland · Lensmen · B. L. Mac Gill
Camera Press · Associated Press · Radio Times Hulton Library

Typesetting (10 on 11 point Melior) 'Monophoto' and
Printed in the Republic of Ireland by John Augustine Ltd, Dublin

Contents

3

EAMON DE VALERA: 1882–1975
Controversial giant of modern Ireland

by Michael McInerney Political Correspondent of THE IRISH TIMES, 1952–1973

Like many great leaders Eamon de Valera began life with even greater obstacles to fame than mere poverty. He was born in a New York tenement area, son of a Spanish music-teacher and of a young Irish woman whose early home had been in a mud cabin in a Limerick village. When little more than two years of age he became virtually an orphan after his father died and his mother found it necessary to send him to her family in Ireland.

Yet Eamon de Valera was to emerge as one of the greatest leaders of the Irish struggle for independence and to achieve international acclaim as President of the League of Nations in the Thirties. The nationalist movement which he inspired and led in Ireland has been acknowledged as that which began the dismantling of the British Empire, giving, as it did, a treasure house of political and guerrilla experience to colonial peoples seeking freedom.

Eamon de Valera in his almost 93 years— from 1882 to 1975—played more roles than Shakespeare's "Seven Ages". After a brief career as a mathematics teacher, he was, in turn, a commandant in the 1916 Easter Rising, a prisoner under death sentence, a reprieved leader of mass prison revolts, and, with only three months' experience in politics, leader of both the Irish Volunteers and Sinn Féin. He was President of the first national parliament, the Dáil; he was outlawed and hunted by his fellow-countrymen only to emerge as leader of the nation's strongest political party, head of the Irish Government, and finally President of the Republic of Ireland.

His undoubted genius for national and international endeavour, however, did not seem to be as effective when, through consummate skill in party politics, he ultimately gained power in Ireland, and was given the opportunity to lift his country in social fields. Nor did that genius help towards some easing of the Northern Question—the plight of the 500,000 Ulster Catholics who were not to know, for 50 years or more, the freedom which had been won for five-sixths of Ireland but who were victims of the power won by Ulster Protestants. In those two spheres his achievements fell far short of his triumphs in purely constitutional and international fields. Perhaps the fault lies not with him only, however, but in the socially and culturally conservative character of the Irish national movement itself, a movement so militant in the measures it adopted to win national sovereignty. Somehow the great principles which he advocated on international issues were not applied to internal affairs in Ireland itself. The two questions of social policy and Ulster policy are closely inter-related and the tragedy of Ireland is that Northern Ireland is even a greater problem today than it was when de Valera set out on his struggle for political independence more than 60 years ago.

Enormity of gains

No other leader achieved so much in establishing Irish nationhood—not Wolfe Tone, not O'Connell, nor Fintan Lalor, the rural genius, nor Michael Davitt with his social revolution, nor Parnell, with his genius and greatness, nor Pearse by his 1916 sacrifice, nor even the Marxist, Connolly, nor Collins, nor Griffith, who were de Valera's partners between 1917 to 1921, though both their promise was stifled in death.

Yet there has never been a full appreciation by the Irish people of the enormity of the gains won between 1917 to 1921, mainly through de Valera's leadership, and during the years 1932 to 1938; nor the achievement of neutrality in the Second World War. Somewhere the heroism of the men of 1916 to 1921, even the magic of the words Irish Republic which

5

Eamon de Valera's parents, Vivion Juan de Valera and Catherine (Kate) Coll, met in New York and were married on September 19, 1881, at St. Patrick's, Greenville, New Jersey. Vivion died in the spring of 1885.

inspired so many was tarnished and faded by tragedy and treachery. Robert Kee, in his magnificent book *The Green Flag* asserted that *"every mystical ideal is diminished by being translated into reality; but that the diminishment in Ireland has been profound."* Perhaps Peguy was nearer: *"What begins as myth ends as politics."*

Are ideals and principles lost when power is won after revolution; are they confounded in the forms of accomplishment? It has happened in so many countries. In Ireland, of course, in de Valera's time the deepest valley of failure and disillusion was the outbreak of civil war in 1922 following the split in the Sinn Féin movement over the Treaty. The "great diminishing factor" consisted in the reality of former comrades at war with each other only a year after

their common victory. It contained the tragic paradox that the Civil War arose from a failure among leaders to agree on the nature of their great triumph. They disagreed on how they could consolidate or further that victory, on what to do with freedom. It was in that darkest hour that de Valera showed sheer political genius in recovering from his own debacle and getting the country to move forward again to complete the national sovereignty for his part of Ireland.

Born in New York

There was some paradox, light and shade even, about Eamon de Valera's birth and youth which had its own international aspects. His Irish mother, the young Catherine Coll, and his Spanish father, Vivion de Valera, had first met

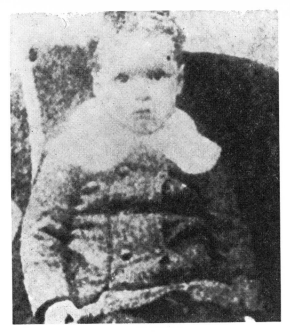

The earliest authenticated photograph of Eamon de Valera, aged 2½.

The certificate of his baptism in New York in December, 1882.

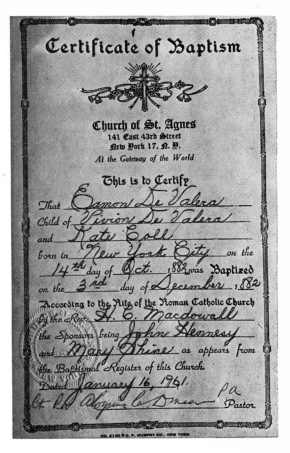

in 1880 in the home of a French family in New York, where Catherine was a domestic. They were married on September 19, 1881, in Greenville, New Jersey, and their only child, registered as George and christened Edward at the baptismal ceremony in the local Catholic church, was to become famous as Eamon de Valera.

There was a paradox in the number of nations involved in his birth and also in the fact that this most famous Irishman was born 3,000 miles away from the land in which he was to achieve such distinction, and that his father was foreign to that land. But then the Irish seem to prefer foreign blood or nationality in their leaders. De Valera was no different in that respect to Wolfe Tone, to Robert Emmet, to Parnell, to Pearse, to Tom Clarke, to James Connolly, to James Larkin, the great Labour leader, or even Liam Mellows, the radical Republican. To be born 3,000 miles away from

Ireland in what was virtually a slum area of New York, and to have had a Spanish father, was hardly an auspicious start to an auspicious life.

De Valera had, however, little time to be even aware of his foreign and unusual origin. He had only the faintest memory of his mother and father in New York. In 1885 he was taken to his grandmother's home, to a small farm in West Limerick, by his uncle Edward Coll. There he received devoted love and kindness from his grandmother and her family until, 14 years later, he left that home to further his education in Blackrock College, Co. Dublin. His mother remarried and paid only occasional visits to her son in Ireland, but kept in constant touch and helped him all she could.

The frugal years

The young de Valera began his education at the Bruree national school and he was very

*His grandmother,
Mrs. Elizabeth Coll, who
looked after him at Bruree
until her death in 1895.*

promising. His grandmother had died in 1895 and his Uncle Patrick was easily won over to the idea that though he could not afford secondary school fees, the young de Valera should go on to the Christian Brothers in Charleville where he hoped to win a university scholarship. He showed something of his future stamina in walking seven miles a day back to Knockmore from Charleville and at the same time helping on the small farm after school-hours. A train took him to Charleville from Bruree, but there was no return train. He is also said to have shown something, even then, of the subtlety in thought and tactics which enabled him to overcome future problems, such as being forced to take an oath to enter the Dáil 30 years later. A school-friend walking home with young Eamon one day had eaten some of the bread which he had bought for his mother, and was worried at the beating he might receive from her for his 'crime'. The young de Valera solved the problem. He handed his friend the bread which he also had bought, and some of which he also had eaten, and suggested that the two should exchange loaves. "You can tell your mother that you didn't eat the bread and you won't be telling a lie" he said. Of course, he too could do the same!

The years in Knockmore and Bruree were years of the barely frugal comfort which he envisaged for a future Ireland many years later; but they were happy years too. West Limerick has its own beauty and history. He made many journeys to and from Limerick city: he so often recalled in later life of driving a pony-driven farm-cart, a country boy with a cap, standing up with the milk cans rattling through Limerick's main streets. On these journeys he would have glimpsed the "lordly Shannon" on its way to the Atlantic, and seen "across Old Shannon's tide, once more the hills of Clare", a county to which he was to bring such fame, and which brought such fame to him.

The Land War

It was in west Limerick too that he developed his extraordinary physical strength and also that devoutness which was such a remarkable influence on his philosophy, character and politics. For it was there he learned of the Land War, as well as religion, from the parish priest, Father Eugene Sheehy, who was, even then, a leader in the struggle of Davitt and Parnell: the young de Valera was growing up between 1885 and Parnell's fall in 1891. He would have heard, too, in those early years of the massacre

8

The burial of Charles Stewart Parnell at Glasnevin in October, 1891. A Protestant landowner and man of exceptional gifts, he led the Irish Party at Westminster, dedicated to the cause of Home Rule; he was acknowledged as the "uncrowned king" of Ireland. Involvement in a divorce action in 1890 brought about his downfall and split his party and supporters across the nation.

John Redmond (top hat), leader of the Irish Party, and Joseph Devlin inspecting National Volunteers at Phoenix Park in 1915.

Labour disputes in Dublin in 1913 culminated in a series of work stoppages. A mass rally of striking tramway workers on August 31 was baton-charged by the police. Scores of people were injured and two men and a woman killed.

Young Dubliners at play near Liberty Hall in 1913 imitated their unemployed fathers who joined the Citizen Army, in the wake of the bitter labour unrest and lock-outs.

at the meeting in Mitchelstown in 1887, and of William O'Brien, John Dillon and others who were then Ireland's political leaders. The land war even penetrated to his own village where a local landlord was the subject of some aggressive attention. His Uncle Pat's membership of Davitt's Land and Labour League may have made him aware of social problems.

But even in those early years he was to take important decisions. Though he willingly tended cattle, cleaning out the byres or doing other work on his uncle's farm he did not intend to spend his life at it, and early on grasped the central idea that a good education was the necessary preliminary to the good and fulfilling life. And he worked hard at Charleville and in any spare time at home, loving his life in rural Ireland, but determined to get out of it. He won a scholarship at Charleville which was to give him secondary education in Blackrock College, Co. Dublin.

In later years he often spoke of his first day in Dublin in September, 1898, not yet 16 years of age, dressed in his new suit which cost 16 shillings and taking a horse-tram from Kingsbridge Station to O'Connell Bridge, and walking much of the four miles from there to Blackrock.

Issues of the day

He almost certainly would have been aware that during that year the centenary of the United Irishmen and Wolfe Tone was being celebrated, that seven years after the death of Parnell, the 'uncrowned king of Ireland', efforts were being made to re-unite the sundered and disgraced Irish Party so as to win Home Rule for Ireland. That year, 1898, local government was introduced and further land legislation conceived, which would affect his own people at Knockmore. But he would hardly have known that about that time Tom Clarke and other Fenians were being released from jails and planning to return to Ireland with renewed determination to plan a revolt against the great British Empire, and secure Ireland's freedom.

Other issues which were to be of later significance were in the air. The Boer War was threatening and was to involve his future close friend, Erskine Childers; Arthur Griffith was returning to Ireland to found Sinn Féin; Connolly's *Workers' Republic* was on sale in the streets, Yeats and Lady Gregory and the Fay Brothers were busy with a national theatre, producing plays that were to be famous. Above all, as he had learned some of the Irish language at home, he would have been aware that a Gaelic League had been formed, just five years before. In that Dublin of horse-trams and cabs events were taking shape which were to bear a profound influence on de Valera's destiny:

His uncles, Pat Coll (left) who brought up the young de Valera at Bruree, and Edward Coll who brought him from New York to the family cottage in Co. Limerick.

11

Childhood portraits: Visits to the photographer in Limerick were made when he was aged 4½ and again at 12 years.

Home Rule and Unionist opposition to its implementation, the fall of Parnell, the strikes and lock-outs, the poverty, the emergence of the Citizen Army, and the inability of the British administration to recognise Ireland's problems.

University studies

Pursuing his goal of further education young Eamon de Valera went to Blackrock College, winning further scholarships to ease his way to university and securing a degree in mathematics from the Royal University. He did post-graduate work after the foundation of University College, Dublin, one of the constituent colleges of National University he was to serve as Chancellor of the N.U.I. for more than 50 years) and also at Trinity College, Dublin. To help him with his expenses of study he gave "grinds" at Blackrock. He secured his first full-time appointment at Rockwell College, Co. Tipperary, and, in 1906, became professor in the women's training college for teachers at Carysfort, Co. Dublin, a post which he left only to take part in the Easter Rising ten years later.

But, a young man with such enormous energy derived from his life in west Limerick, could not be content with study only and he became active in rugby football, in athletics, in cycling and other sports, discovering probably early in life that an active mind needs a healthy body. It was a practice which he never lost throughout his long life, and it gave him an energy with which even three of his security guards on eight-hour shifts found it difficult to cope, even in his sixties.

But now that his formal studies were completed and his career as a teacher decided on, the 25-year-old de Valera found time to study the language in which he had become interested at home, and in 1908, he took what was to be a decisive step. He joined the Gaelic League, never dreaming that it would lead to fame. Not content with the progress he was making there he became a student at the Leinster College of Irish where the young teacher, Sinéad O'Flanagan, enthralled him. He won her affections against keen competition from all the rest of her male class who already were in love with her beauty, her charm and her gifts of intelligence. Eamon and Sinéad were married two years later, on January 8, 1910, in St. Paul's Catholic Church, Arran Quay, Dublin.

Ceremony in Irish

The happy couple more or less conducted the ceremony in Irish themselves as the priest did not know the language and needed prompting. And so it was that though his fate was decided by joining the Gaelic League, where he was to meet men like Pearse and MacDonagh, then active in the Irish Republican Brotherhood, he had actually married and founded a family before he became embroiled in national politics. His married life was very happy to the end. When she was 96 and dying in January 1975, he at 92 visited her daily to hold her hand and sing in Irish to her. They died within eight months of the other.

In 1912–14, the Home Rule struggle assumed crisis proportions with Tory opposition to the proposal, the curtailment of the Lords' veto, the support among Liberals for Home Rule and the grim resistance of Northern Unionists which was expressed forcibly in the formation of the Ulster Volunteer Force, the Larne gun-running by the U.V.F. and the vehemence of the rejection of Home Rule by Edward Carson, the new Unionist leader. De Valera was certainly stirred by all this and when a mass meeting was called in November 1913, to launch an army of Irish Volunteers in a new national movement, he was among the first to fill up the recruiting form after serious consideration of family responsibility. He had taken a fateful step. Soon he was attending arms drill, and successively became a lieutenant, captain, and commandant of the Third Battalion of the Dublin Brigade, and later still, adjutant of the Dublin Brigade. He was meeting Padraic Pearse, Thomas MacDonagh and Tom Clarke, the leaders of the Republican Brotherhood who decided that a Rising against the British would take place before the Great War ended.

Opposed to I.R.B. secrecy

Now, however, there was an incident which revealed something of the mind of de Valera. MacDonagh asked him to join the Irish Republican Brotherhood, the secret revolutionary body formed in 1858 by James Stephens, and which carried out the abortive Fenian Rising of 1867. The I.R.B. had been re-organised by

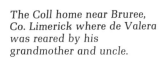

The Coll home near Bruree, Co. Limerick where de Valera was reared by his grandmother and uncle.

The young de Valera (left at back) with fellow pupils and Brother Prendeville, head teacher, at Charleville school in the summer of 1898.

Pearse, Clarke, Seán MacDermott and others, and MacDonagh urged its effectiveness to de Valera.

At first he refused bluntly to join. It was against his judgement to join a body so subject to secret orders from unknown men, but, because he was becoming aware that some of his own juniors in the Volunteers were in possession of more military information than he, agreed to join formally; but he refused to attend any secret meetings. It says something for de Valera, however, that in spite of this decision his own company was the only section of the Volunteers which opted by majority to remain with the original MacNeill Volunteers, after Redmond's famous speech in Woodenbridge, Co. Wicklow, in 1914 pledging Volunteer support for the British war effort; the company, however, later dwindled to almost nothing. At that time Redmond had popular support.

As Easter 1916 approached de Valera was informed by MacDonagh of the plans for the Rebellion, and, though he expressed his disagreement with the tactics planned, he obeyed, "as a soldier", he said, MacDonagh's orders, and undertook his military command and duties. The story of de Valera's part in that Rising has been told many times and is well known. His command orders were to guard the south-eastern approaches to the city, to hamper British troops advancing from Dun Laoghaire (Kingstown) or from Beggar's Bush Barracks. He had known this for some time and had studied his area with mathematical thoroughness.

Enterprising commander
He proved to be courageous, efficient and enterprising, devising what might have been the original tank in the form of a specially-loaded train which was to effect some destruction to the nearby railway lines. He, like Pearse, MacDonagh, Clarke, and Connolly, had ignored the order from the Volunteers' Commanding Officer, Eoin MacNeill, countermanding the call of the I.R.B. Military Council for the Rising on Easter Sunday. MacNeill's action, however,

Eamon de Valera (circled) as a 16-year-old pupil at Blackrock College in 1898, and (below) as an exhibitioner who obtained honours in Greek, Latin, French, Arithmetic, Algebra, and Euclid, and a pass in Trigonometry.

Edward De Valera

Retained Exhibition, £30. Book Prize, £2. *Hon.* Greek, Latin, French, Arithmetic, Algebra, Euclid. *Pass* Trigonometry.

After the conferring of his degree in mathematics at the Royal University in 1904.

15

Eamon de Valera
and Sinéad
Ní Fhlannagain on
the day of their
wedding, January 8,
1910, at St. Paul's
Church, Arran
Quay, Dublin.

reduced de Valera's forces, like those of other leaders, to a pitifully small number. Yet he held out in his headquarters at Boland's Mills, even beyond the call of Pearse after six days, to surrender. His men, in selected outposts had inflicted severe casualties on British troops as they tried to march along Northumberland Road, and other routes, into the city. Though his own casualties were also heavy he was the last Volunteer commandant to surrender his positions. He worked until the surrender order had been confirmed by MacDonagh.

The fact that de Valera was the last to surrender on that historic weekend of April 30, 1916 had the consequence that he was detained at the old Pembroke Town Hall at Ballsbridge instead of in Dublin, thus delaying the courtmartial which awaited him as well as all rebel leaders. That delay may have saved his life: the executions of Pearse, Clarke,

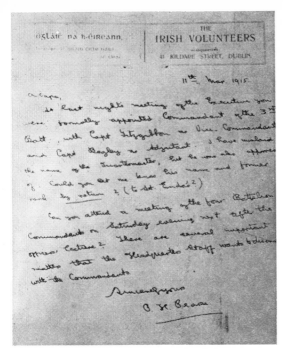

Pearse's letter of March 11, 1915, advising de Valera of his formal appointment as commandant of the Third Dublin Battalion of the Irish Volunteers.

The young commandant whose battalion controlled the south-east approaches to the city by occupation of Boland's bakery and other strategic buildings and thus delayed the British advance on the city centre.

MacDonagh and others, had caused widespread revulsion amongst democratic and liberal minds in Britain as well as in Ireland. George Bernard Shaw was among the first to protest and he was joined by Nationalist leaders like Redmond, and John Dillon. Even Carson, the Unionist leader, tried to call a halt. By May 8 therefore, when de Valera was courtmartialled, a new climate was evolving.

He had no doubt that his death was near; he and his comrades even joked about it. His last letters of farewell were surprisingly cheerful, particularly to Mick Ryan, his old international rugby friend of Rockwell. He was indeed sentenced to death, but almost immediately, he was reprieved. He accepted both the death sentence and the reprieve without any visible emotion. It is of interest that on the same day, W. T. Cosgrave, who was to become the first President of the Free State six years later, was sentenced to death and reprieved.

History was setting the stage for future events.

De Valera (marked X) leading his men under British escort after he was ordered by Pearse to surrender the Volunteers' control of Boland's Mills.

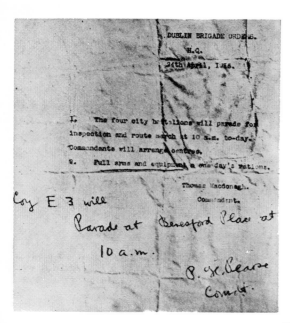

The 1916 Rising mobilisation order
which superseded MacNeill's
cancellation of a previous order.

POBLACHT NA H EIREANN.
THE PROVISIONAL GOVERNMENT
OF THE
IRISH REPUBLIC
TO THE PEOPLE OF IRELAND.

IRISHMEN AND IRISHWOMEN: In the name of God and of the dead generations from which she receives her old tradition of nationhood, Ireland, through us, summons her children to her flag and strikes for her freedom.

Having organised and trained her manhood through her secret revolutionary organisation, the Irish Republican Brotherhood, and through her open military organisations, the Irish Volunteers and the Irish Citizen Army, having patiently perfected her discipline, having resolutely waited for the right moment to reveal itself, she now seizes that moment, and, supported by her exiled children in America and by gallant allies in Europe, but relying in the first on her own strength, she strikes in full confidence of victory.

We declare the right of the people of Ireland to the ownership of Ireland, and to the unfettered control of Irish destinies, to be sovereign and indefeasible. The long usurpation of that right by a foreign people and government has not extinguished the right, nor can it ever be extinguished except by the destruction of the Irish people. In every generation the Irish people have asserted their right to national freedom and sovereignty; six times during the past three hundred years they have asserted it in arms. Standing on that fundamental right and again asserting it in arms in the face of the world, we hereby proclaim the Irish Republic as a Sovereign Independent State, and we pledge our lives and the lives of our comrades-in-arms to the cause of its freedom, of its welfare, and of its exaltation among the nations.

The Irish Republic is entitled to, and hereby claims, the allegiance of every Irishman and Irishwoman. The Republic guarantees religious and civil liberty, equal rights and equal opportunities to all its citizens, and declares its resolve to pursue the happiness and prosperity of the whole nation and of all its parts, cherishing all the children of the nation equally, and oblivious of the differences carefully fostered by an alien government, which have divided a minority from the majority in the past.

Until our arms have brought the opportune moment for the establishment of a permanent National Government, representative of the whole people of Ireland and elected by the suffrages of all her men and women, the Provisional Government, hereby constituted, will administer the civil and military affairs of the Republic in trust for the people.

We place the cause of the Irish Republic under the protection of the Most High God, Whose blessing we invoke upon our arms, and we pray that no one who serves that cause will dishonour it by cowardice, inhumanity, or rapine. In this supreme hour the Irish nation must, by its valour and discipline and by the readiness of its children to sacrifice themselves for the common good, prove itself worthy of the august destiny to which it is called.

Signed on Behalf of the Provisional Government,

THOMAS J. CLARKE,
SEAN Mac DIARMADA,   THOMAS MacDONAGH,
P. H. PEARSE,   EAMONN CEANNT,
JAMES CONNOLLY.   JOSEPH PLUNKETT.

The 1916 Proclamation: the document issued by the Provisional Government during the Rising, proclaiming the Irish Republic.

De Valera under close arrest before his courtmartial in 1916. He, Thomas Ashe and W. T. Cosgrave were later reprieved the firing squad.

British troops trying to dislodge snipers during the Rising.

The G.P.O. in the aftermath of the British attack on the 1916 insurgents. Pearse and the survivors were forced to evacuate and surrender after four days of continuous shelling, principally by the gunboat Helga moored in the Liffey.

The combined garrisons of Cumann na mBan who assisted the men of 1916. They acted as messengers, scouts and first aid nurses during the seven-day Rising. Irish Volunteers (below), with only bandoliers and haversacks to distinguish them from civilians, parading at Fairview in Dublin before the Rising. Arthur Griffith, who became first President of the Irish Free State and who died in 1922, is shown fourth from the right.

The main thoroughfare and its environs in Dublin reduced to ruins after six days of fighting during the 1916 Rising.

The emblazoned green flag which was run up over the G.P.O. at 3 o'clock on the afternoon of Easter Monday, 1916.

The emergent politician

Eamon de Valera's first role, that of soldier, was completed when the Easter Rising ended after six days, but those six days proved to be the launching pad for a long future career almost exclusively confined to politics.

After reprieve came a role as jail leader, when he, with thousands of others, was imprisoned in England. His gift for political leadership was to be demonstrated initially, of all places, among the 65 volunteer prisoners who were jailed with him in Dartmoor. As one of the two surviving Commandants of the Rising (Thomas Ashe who died a year later, was the other) de Valera could exert his military authority as senior commandant, naturally, but one of many incidents, illustrates his political mind.

One morning while the prisoners were lined up for inspection they noticed Eoin MacNeill, their former commander leading a group of new prisoners coming down the steps into the dark central hall of Dartmoor Prison. The prisoners had mixed feelings about MacNeill because of his attempt to ban the mobilisation for the Rising. As MacNeill arrived, de Valera, to the amazement of all, stepped out in front of his men and ordered, in ringing tones: "Irish Volunteers! Attention! Eyes left!" The men responded to the order with extra military precision, for MacNeill was still, formally, their commanding officer. Not alone was he being accepted, but honoured. The act, which risked the penalty of flogging for de Valera, had many facets. It showed de Valera's gift for quick decision and action, and above all, a political percipience about the future pattern of Irish politics. All who believed in Irish independence, in whatever form, would be needed in the new movement which even then, de Valera was envisaging. The short-term aim was to preserve internal unity in the prison. (The story is told by Robert Brennan and is included in Dorothy Macardle's *Irish Republic*.)

Despite their rankings, however, it was de Valera, and not MacNeill, who became the unquestioned leader of the prisoners in the various and ingenious forms of protest and courageous demands for status as political prisoners and for better prison conditions. That prison prestige had its own importance when the prisoners began to be released. After hundreds of the less important prisoners, including Collins, had been released in December 1916, the leaders, including de Valera were released six months later, in June 1917, as Lloyd George launched the Irish Convention in an attempt to solve the Irish Question.

Change in outlook

Those releases were to evoke a response which showed that the outlook of the people of Ireland had changed utterly since Easter 1916. Then, as they had been marched away to jail, the insurgents were jeered and insulted by the people of Dublin. Now the first batch of released prisoners were welcomed home by cheering thousands and bonfires blazed all over Ireland. By the summer of 1917 that change had intensified and de Valera, as the obvious senior commandant, was accepted as something special by the crowd on his arrival back in Dublin. Again, as bonfires blazed all over the country, it was announced that de Valera was to be the Volunteers' candidate for the parliamentary by-election in East Clare. The vacancy was caused by the death on a French battlefield of its M.P.—Major Willie Redmond, brother of John Redmond, the Irish Party leader.

There was plenty of support for his nomination. Something very new was clearly stirring in Ireland. The Easter Rising martyrs had become national heroes: songs and ballads were being composed and sung, and their pictures were being sold in thousands. Those leaders who had survived were not neglected and de Valera's picture too, was becoming familiar. Thousands were joining, first the new organisation espoused by Kathleen Clarke, widow of Tom Clarke, the 1916 signatory, the Prisoners' Aid and other such funds which had varied activities to keep Republicans in touch. The change had been helped also by the anger over the continuation of martial law, the hanging of Sir Roger Casement in August, the policy of continuous arrests of sympathisers of the Easter Rising, by the report of the Royal Commission into the Rising, and by the report on the murder of Francis Sheehy Skeffington, a leading pacifist and socialist: the report proved that Captain Bowen-Colthurst who had shot him, was guilty but insane. There were hints also that conscription might be applied to Ireland. The release of the prisoners in December and in the following June had fuelled the fire rather than damped it down.

Now the militarism of Easter Week was to usher in the greatest political movement that Ireland had ever known. On the day of his arrival home de Valera showed his political drive. He was the first signatory to a cable to the United States President hailing Wilson's call that every nation had the right to self-determination and urging him to apply that principle to Ireland.

Election strategy

That very first political act was a hint that de Valera was very much alive, even on that testing and busy day, to the importance of international action.

De Valera exploited the new Easter Week feeling to the utmost. There had been already

June 17, 1917, de Valera coming down the gangplank at Dun Laoghaire with other prisoners released in England.

Sinn Féin by-election victories in Roscommon and Longford; now de Valera led a whirlwind campaign in Clare. He united his support first by declaring that his aim was that of the Easter Week men. He reunited the pre-1916 men insisting, against opposition, that Eoin MacNeill, the Volunteers' former commanding officer, should appear on his platform in Clare. His first rough formula for unity—the aim of the Republic but ultimately a people's decision on the form of the Irish State—was that which, a few months later, created a whole new and dynamic movement. It also helped towards the massive win he registered in East Clare, an event that was celebrated throughout the country, demonstrating decisively the profound change in Irish politics. A further success was recorded when W. T. Cosgrave achieved a big victory in Kilkenny a month later. Lloyd George's

Irish Convention, set up to seek Irish agreement on Home Rule but boycotted by Sinn Féin and Labour, now seemed—and was to become—doomed. In contrast de Valera was greeted everywhere, already, as the national leader. He spent almost every weekend speaking to mass-meetings of Volunteers.

Those months of the summer and autumn of 1917 saw most exciting events. In his 35th year, and despite having a young family, he abandoned teaching and set himself the task of merging all the independence forces into one great united body. He became a full-time organiser and was given an allowance. An earlier effort at unity by Count Plunkett in April 1917 had failed. It did, however, set up a council representing 70 organisations including the Volunteers, Sinn Féin, the I.R.B., Liberty Clubs,

Citizens Army, Labour groups and other bodies. It was only a liaison council for discussion and decision and by no means a united group.

Campaign for unity

That Council met, with de Valera and other leading former prisoners present for the first time, and appointed a committee to establish national aims to be set before a planned ard-fheis in October, 1917. De Valera saw this committee as a most important key in his bid to form one unified organisation of all who supported independence. He had some success at unity in Clare, and while the funeral of Thomas Ashe, who had died on hunger strike, aroused a united demonstration, there was much to do yet to get one united body.

Jubilation in East Clare, 1917: de Valera, in the uniform of a Volunteers' officer, hearing of his election as a Sinn Féin member. He represented the constituency for 42 years up to 1959. The first election poster (below) published by his agent.

WE GOT HIM OUT
TO PUT HIM IN
VOTE FOR DE VALERA,
A FELON OF OUR LAND.

At Croke Park on April 6, 1919, when Wexford and Tipperary met in football to raise funds for republican prisoners, de Valera with Arthur Griffith, Larry O'Neill, Lord Mayor of Dublin, and Michael Collins.
De Valera threw in the ball to start the game. The referee (right) was *Harry Boland*.

De Valera told this writer many years later of the bitterness and distrust that existed and developed as that first meeting of the new committee proceeded: *At one stage all seemed lost when Cathal Brugha, Sean Milroy, and Rory O'Connor strongly denounced Sinn Féin and the three of them were walking out of the meeting at 6 Harcourt Street, Dublin. I called on them to come back, that I had something important to say and that it held out the hope of agreement. They did come back and I then proposed a new formula for unity.* That 'magical formula', as F. S. L. Lyons has described it, was: *Sinn Féin aims at securing international recognition of Ireland as an independent Irish Republic; having achieved that status the Irish people may, by referendum, choose their own form of Government.* De Valera, in his later comment to me, said: *I knew that this could not mean anything else but the Republic, for we had no descendants of the O'Neills or the O'Donnells or other princes, claiming the throne of Ireland.*

That proposal transformed the meeting from one of unrest to unanimous approval of the new aims. It was, indeed, extraordinarily ingenious. To urge the conservatives of the old Sinn Féin to seek an Irish Republic and to get their consent was one 'miracle', but to get the militant volunteers like Brugha to accept the name "Sinn Féin" was even an achievement for the bitterness between them was very deep. The media had tried to ridicule Easter Week by dubbing it as the "Sinn Féin" Rising, as already Sinn Féin was associated with extremism.

And yet that very formula, though it was approved unanimously and with much enthusiasm by the ard-fheis a few weeks later, held within itself the future disastrous split. De Valera, elected President of Sinn Féin at the ard-fheis, even told the 1,700 delegates, that acceptance of the new aims to secure unity, would leave them free to "agree to differ afterwards" about the forms of Government of the nation.

He was unanimously accepted by all groups, rising above men of wide and long experience of politics like Arthur Griffith, W. T. Cosgrave, Seán T. O'Kelly, and others. He was still quite young compared with Griffith and much younger-looking, almost studentish with his pale face, dark hair and glasses.

Collins and the I.R.B.

Griffith had stood down for that Presidential election, describing de Valera as "a soldier and a statesman", surely the supreme tribute paid to one who had entered politics but a few months. Count Plunkett, father of Joseph Plunkett, the 1916 martyr, also stood down in the same election. In his presidential speech, however, de Valera, to clinch the support of the Volunteer representatives present, stressed the aim "Republic", a factor which must have caused Griffith some uneasiness. But the speech won the day and the new Sinn Féin was born. De Valera, too, insisted that Eoin MacNeill should be a member of the new executive.

But there was one serious snag in the harmony of the new organisation. Michael Collins who had been elected at the bottom of the poll at the ard-fheis, and who was almost unknown until the Ashe funeral where he said a few militant words at the graveside, had been organising the Irish Republican Brotherhood, both in Frongoch and since his release in December, 1916.

The I.R.B. was now a powerful organisation, but secret, and as it grew, its members penetrated into Sinn Féin and the Volunteers, securing high positions: Collins himself was appointed as director of organisation of the Volunteers, other I.R.B. members being secretary and director of communications. Collins was also a member of the Sinn Féin executive, his inclusion had been urged by de Valera. But, as all other organisations merged into the new Sinn Féin, the I.R.B. remained apart, taking separate decisions and retaining a great deal of control over the Army. It had, of course, the prestige of being the organisation which had organised and carried through the Easter Week Rising. All the signatories to the Proclamation had been leading I.R.B. members.

De Valera himself had thought out and had written the constitution rules, and form of structure of both the Volunteers and of Sinn Féin. Both organisations had military characteristics of army headquarters and executive and staff or party executive, brigades, battalions, companies and sections or, in the political party sense, party headquarters and executive, regional, county, parish or cumainn. *"The Army were citizen soldiers"*, he told me *"and great numbers of them were also members of Sinn Féin executives, clubs and of the Sinn Féin Executive. I was President of both Sinn Féin and the army."* Fianna Fáil, he said, was built in 1926 on the same military basis.

But after that ard-fheis the division between de Valera and the I.R.B. widened and became embittered. That division had been extended at the ard-fheis where the I.R.B. had opposed MacNeill while de Valera had supported him. Collins had also produced a list of I.R.B. members whom he wanted elected on the executive, and its discovery caused anger, resulting in Collins himself being the last to be elected.

Severance with I.R.B.
Now, came a remarkable and significant development in tactics and strategy by de Valera. Though wearing his banned Easter Week uniform, everywhere proclaiming his eternal allegiance to the men of Easter Week and its Proclamation, he ignored and rejected the strategy and tactics of the organisers of the Rising.

He pointedly severed his own connection with the I.R.B. though that connection had been merely formal, and he advised his closest associates, like Cathal Brugha, to do the same. But Austin Stack and Harry Boland, who were both close to de Valera and Seán T. O'Kelly, continued their membership, and kept de Valera informed of decisions (indeed, it was through them he learned, in 1921, that Collins would accept the Crown). He rejected the I.R.B. secrecy, its danger in the sense that meant divided councils and commands, a division which had caused havoc in 1916 and which was to do so again in 1922. In addition, its secrecy was condemned by the Catholic Church whose support he wanted.

Instead of the Easter Week tactics, he wanted to fuse all the forms of a century's revolutions into a single stream which the people would identify with and which would identify with the people and involve them, which would be secret to the British but open to the Irish. Above all it would not be a conspiracy. It would use all forms of struggle, and though it would use physical force, it could control such force.

But that split between de Valera and the I.R.B. marked the beginning of suspicion between

Addressing an election meeting in 1918.

de Valera and Collins, who soon became President of the I.R.B. supreme council, and therefore, in I.R.B. terms, President of the Republic. Cathal Brugha, now no longer a member of the I.R.B., had been elected chief-of-staff of the Army, and later Minister for Defence in the first Government of the Republic elected by the First Dáil. Here again began the intense antagonism between Brugha and Collins.

Meanwhile, de Valera continued his open campaign, declaring his aim to be "to make British Government impossible in Ireland". His speeches disturbed Lloyd George, British Prime Minister: *"They are plain deliberate, almost cold-blooded incitements to rebellion . . . It is a case of a man of great ability, of considerable influence . . . deliberately stirring up people to rebellion . . ."*

Soon there were Sinn Féin clubs in every parish. De Valera saw an election coming at some time in the future, and he wanted to use Sinn Féin to secure a mandate for his policy of sovereign independence.

Bonus of conscription

Such activities and policies meant new election victories, though in Waterford—when John Redmond died, perhaps broken by the inevitable failure of the Irish Convention, caused by the withdrawal from him of the support of Bishop O'Donnell—the Sinn Féin candidate was defeated. Sinn Féin was defeated also in East Tyrone, but Griffith who, along with MacNeill, did not take part in the Rising, won in Cavan.

Once again the British came to the aid of de Valera, when in April 1918 Lloyd George announced that conscription would apply to Ireland. The threat won Cavan for Sinn Féin: it had been there vaguely since 1916, and had aided Sinn Féin and the Volunteers, and now recruits poured into all Republican bodies. Again de Valera was to take the lead in uniting all forces, even the Church and the Nationalist Party, Labour and all his own organisations. He drafted the pledge to be taken at all chapel gates against conscription and a Mansion House meeting of all parties, supported the draft. The pledge said: *"We pledge ourselves to resist conscription by the most effective means at our disposal"*, a form of words which could mean different things to different people. But it worked. In a declaration passed at the meeting de Valera said that the Conscription Act would *"be a declaration of war on the Irish nation"*.

The extent of de Valera's drive against conscription was demonstrated by a general strike of many workers and all over Ireland, except in the North, everything stopped. It was repeated in 1920 in protest against treatment of prisoners, but in both cases it was a strike by an entire community. Those strikes illustrated the links between Labour and the Republican movement, leaders from Labour being in close touch with de Valera. The threat of conscription remained until the Armistice of November, 1918, but by that time de Valera and many other leaders were back in jail in England.

When, after the Armistice, Lloyd George called a general election in December 1918, there

De Valera and John Dillon at an anti-Conscription meeting in Ballaghderreen, Co. Roscommon, in 1918. Dillon succeeded John Redmond as leader of the Irish Party.

were 1,200 Sinn Féin clubs and over 100,000 Volunteers throughout the country. The conscription issue was probably one of the more important factors in the inevitable victory of Sinn Féin. They won 73 out of the 105 seats in an election which gave the vote to a new generation and votes for women for the first time on the same basis as the franchise had been extended in Britain.

De Valera saw at once the opportunity which that 1918 election gave to revolutionary Ireland. He had no scruples in using British systems to secure an Irish Republican victory. And he ensured that the Labour Party, which had been founded by Connolly and Larkin in 1912, made the great sacrifice in yielding to his and other pleadings to stand aside in the election so that the "national will" could be declared without qualification.

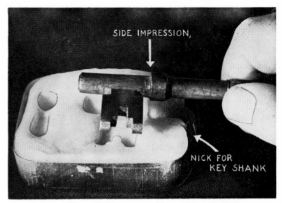

De Valera effected his escape from Lincoln Jail in February, 1919, by surrepticiously making a wax impression of the key used by the prison chaplain. A drawing of the key's dimension was sent to Ireland under the guise of a Christmas card and after several setbacks blank keys were finally smuggled in a cake into the Irish prisoners.

Nationalists crushed

In the election the Unionists secured 26 seats, eight extra, demonstrating new fears of a United Ireland. The Irish Parliamentary Party was completely wiped out, securing only six seats—five in the North—out of the 80 it held before the election. Waterford returned a Redmond, and Joe Devlin defeated de Valera in Belfast. De Valera was returned unopposed in East Clare and defeated John Dillon, the Irish Party leader, in East Mayo. The rout was complete. The Sinn Féin triumph was total, except in Ulster. The Unionists had a majority in Antrim, Derry, Down and Armagh, but were a minority in Tyrone and Fermanagh, and altogether they polled 315,394 votes, about a fifth of the total electorate. All in England and Ireland, and even Unionist Ulster, admitted that voters in Catholic Ireland had given an unqualified mandate for independence. But that Northern resistance, small though it appeared, was to prove to be a major stumbling block to an all-Ireland Republic.

Collins and Brugha and others, in the absence of de Valera and Griffith in jail, began the organising of the first historic Dáil. In that organising was disclosed the inherently conservative character of the Irish revolution, for there was disagreement with the Social Programme drafted by Labour men, Cathal O'Shannon, Bill O'Brien and Tom Johnson. It had contained some social revolutionary phrases like *"no private right to property against the public right of the nation",* words which Patrick Lynch has pointed out, were taken from Patrick Pearse's *Sovereign People,* and also the phrase *"the nation must ever retain the right to resume possession of such soil or wealth whenever the trust is abused or the trustee fails to give faithful service."*

Collins, sometimes thought of as a radical, and the I.R.B. were appalled at the first draft and, according to James Ryan, later to be a de Valera Minister, Seán T. O'Kelly stayed up all night at his (Ryan's) sister's house in Rathmines, Dublin, rewriting the Johnson-O'Shannon draft. Later de Valera denigrated the programme in the Dáil, revealing his own social outlook.

The first Dáil of 1919 concentrated more on national rather than social revolution. The attendance numbered not more than 27 of the elected 73 members. The five Nationalist M.P.s from the North ignored the invitation to take their seats, 34 other members, including de Valera and Griffith, were imprisoned in Britain. Collins also did not attend; another eight or so were unable to accept the invitation. The new parliament ratified the Republic declared in Easter 1916, promulgated the watered down social programme, and referred to "the existing state of war between Ireland and England". The words were truer than they knew for at the same time Volunteers under Dan Breen opened

The First Dáil Eireann met in the Mansion House on January 21, 1919.

hostilities in Tipperary that were to last for just two years.

Escape from Lincoln

On February 3, 1919, less than a fortnight after that First Dáil meeting, there came a dramatic change when de Valera, imprisoned in Lincoln Jail since May 1918, made a dramatic escape, astonishing the British, and setting the Irish hills ablaze.

With a general release of prisoners shortly afterwards de Valera took his place in the Dáil and at a Sinn Féin ard-fheis. At both he was ratified as President, and appointed a well-balanced Government, and discussed the efforts of Seán T. O'Kelly and others to secure recognition of Irish rights of self-determination at the Paris Peace Conference. But first he insisted that the position of the Dáil, the Government and the Army should be cleared up. In the Dáil he asserted the Government's full control of the Army (the I.R.A. as it was popularly known). *The Army is a regular State force under civilian control of the elected representatives, and is operated by officers appointed by the Minister for Defence in the Government."*

De Valera, supported by Griffith and the rest of the Cabinet, now held that the recognition of Ireland's sovereignty by the Great Powers at the Versailles Peace Conference must become an international issue. De Valera, it was decided, should go to the United States and lead the movement developing there urging President Wilson to secure recognition of the Irish Republic and to raise an external loan by means of bonds to assist the new Republic.

Before leaving Ireland de Valera declared his aims. Ireland, free and sovereign, would be prepared to enter a League of Nations and contribute freely her gifts to the world and receive back the gifts which other democratic nations would contribute to mankind.

He sailed for New York in June, 1919, stowing away in the hold of a Liverpool ship, and entered the United States illegally. He stayed for 18 months or so, secured £6 m. for the Republic Bonds, and helped to raise a further £1 m. otherwise. He spoke at meetings in almost every State, receiving massive welcomes everywhere and great support of many State legislatures and organisations. But he failed to unite the warring American factions and had to take, strong and, at times, ruthless action to force through his policies, at length even to forge his own organisation to raise funds and support.

He failed to move President Wilson or the U.S. Congress, but did receive over 400 votes, against about 700, at the Democratic Party convention on the proposal of recognition. His efforts to secure recognition were hampered by the rival Irish American group of John Devoy, the old Fenian, who later accepted the Treaty, and by Judge Daniel Cohalan.

De Valera's mother when he visited her in the United States in 1919. She married Charles Wheelwright three years after the death of Vivion de Valera in 1885.

Throughout his U.S. visit he stressed self-determination, rather than Republic, but then self-determination was the international issue. He seemed also to compromise in suggesting that Britain conclude a Cuba-style Treaty with Ireland, a Monroe Doctrine arrangement, in that Ireland, if a Republic and free, would be ready to accord Britain some aid if she were attacked. No nation would be able to use Ireland as a base for attack on Britain, but Britain must guarantee first that Irish independence would be granted and preserved. The publication of that idea caused much confusion among the American Irish and also at home, but de Valera was able to defend himself to good effect. It was, perhaps, the first indication of that "external association" formula which later became so famous.

Loan to Russia

In the United States also he entered into negotiations with the Soviet Union to secure recognition of the Republic. Draft terms suggested commercial ideas designed to secure support in Northern Ireland for trade, and, remarkably, the treaty would entrust to accredited representatives of the Irish Republic the interests of the Roman Catholic Church within the territories of the Soviet Republic—quite a concession. It also would have facilitated training for Irish officers on Soviet territory. In New York de Valera lent £25,000 to the Soviet consul receiving, as collateral, a collection of Russian crown jewels. Worth much more, they were returned 28 years later by Paddy McGilligan, the Inter-Party Finance Minister.

That visit to the United States, however, stimulated later the view that de Valera's 18 months there, combined with his six months in jail after Collins had been released in December 1916, and another nine months in Lincoln, had given Michael Collins greater freedom to organise the Irish Republican Brotherhood. That period of June 1919 to December 1920, however, was the period in which Collins's name became a household word as the inspirer and the executor of the military struggle, as the man of iron nerve and of his grim decisions to wipe out the British spy-ring. It was the period, too, of the Collins-Brugha enmity on the issue of Dáil control of the Army. In that period Collins became also a rival to de Valera, a fact which de Valera noted on his

The first bond certificate issued in the United States in January, 1920, as authenticated in de Valera's handwriting.

De Valera with the veteran Fenian leader, John Devoy in New York, 1919, flanked by Harry Boland, Liam Mellows, Padraig McCartan and Diarmuid Lynch.

Driving in triumphal procession in Chicago in 1919 during his 18-month stay in the United States.

return home in December 1920. Collins was acting President after Griffith's arrest, though Brugha stood next to Griffith in seniority. Here again I.R.B. influence was decisive. Collins in everything was first-class, and more, even in his handling of diplomatic overtures from British and other sources about a possible truce or peace talks.

De Valera's influence was still so powerful that he was able to urge successfully a strategic or tactical change in army operations. He insisted that the people were suffering too great a burden from Black-and-Tans reprisals. He was in some conflict with Collins and Dick Mulcahy and the Army H.Q. staff when he outlined a decrease in the number of ambushes, and urged instead large-scale major attacks of sabotage such as the burning down of the Custom House and other centres of adminis-

tration so as to make British government impossible. According to Mulcahy, the Custom House operation was carried out by the Dublin Brigade rather than under the direction of Collins and H.Q. because of disagreement. De Valera claimed it was impossible to beat the British on the ground, but their rule had to be made impossible.

His claim that the people were becoming weary of their sacrifice and hardship could possibly have shown a real perception, and indeed, six months later when the Truce was called and talks began with Britain to seek a settlement, the desire of the people for a lasting peace was made very manifest, and became an overwhelming factor. Historians have claimed that the attacks on the Custom House and other administrative centres were the final blow at British administration.

HALF-BROTHERS: The Rev.
Thomas Wheelwright, C.SS.R.,
shaking hands with his half-
brother during de Valera's visit
to the United States in 1919.
During de Valera's imprisonment in
England Father Wheelwright and
other American Redemptorists
appealed to the U.S. President,
Woodrow Wilson, to intercede
with the British.

Peace overtures

As 1921 advanced, events were moving to a
climax. Approaches from the British side seeking peace became so numerous that de Valera
had to insist that such approaches must be
made direct to him. A factor was that Lloyd
George himself was under internal pressure:
the demand for peace was growing in Britain.

To Labour had been added some of the great
newspapers and journals, national personalities
like the Archbishop of Canterbury, leading
members, even of the House of Lords, writers
like George Bernard Shaw, professors, and
M.P.s, all urging peace. Even Sir Henry Wilson,
so bitter against Ireland, had to say that a
Cabinet plan to send 100,000 troops to Ireland

and to declare martial law, would not succeed because British and Dominion opinion would disapprove strongly. The Irish were winning the propaganda battle.

In May, 1921, came the declaration of two general elections. They were to select the new Parliament for Northern Ireland and Southern Ireland under the terms of the Government of Ireland Act of 1920. De Valera's decision to use the election as a further demonstration of the Irish desire for sovereignty, caused immediate alarm among some Republicans who saw the decision as a recognition of Partition. In the event none need have worried because in the South all the 128 Republican candidates were returned unopposed, hardly a demonstration of the will of the people, rather a demonstration of the strength of Sinn Féin. But that Second Dáil was to decide the Treaty decision eight months later. In the North the Unionists won 40 of the 52 seats, the Nationalists 12—an election which demonstrated an opposite strength to that of the South. The election in the South was held on the very day that the Partition Act became law. The new Viceroy, Lord Fitzalan, took up office in the Viceregal Lodge. He was not to stay very long.

On May 5, 1921, before the general election, a meeting was arranged between Sir James Craig, the Unionist leader, and de Valera in the belief that some agreement might be possible along the lines of a Council of Ireland. Craig was taken to meet de Valera by a senior I.R.A. officer, Emmet Dalton, but the meeting ended in deadlock. Official historians claim that each man had been led to believe that the other had expressed a wish for consultation.

Ernest Blythe, one of de Valera's Ministers, however, told the present writer that de Valera had reported to his Cabinet that Craig had proposed that a settlement could be reached along the lines of two Dominion States in Ireland —North and South—and that a Council of Ireland could be set up to decide on mutual problems. He also, according to Blythe, had declared that the proposal had the support of Winston Churchill. De Valera reported to the Cabinet that he had turned down the proposal as utterly unsatisfactory. It would have meant, of course, an abandonment of the Republic, and instead implied membership of the British

Michael Collins and Diarmuid O'Hegarty opening subscriptions for the Dáil Eireann first internal loan, 1919.

Commonwealth. To Blythe it was *"a great opportunity for settlement, missed"*.

Meeting Lloyd George
Clearly, however, Lloyd George had other ideas and as pressure mounted in Britain for a settlement, as his own internal problems grew, with serious industrial unrest, he settled on some form of self-government for "that part of Ireland which demanded it", but of a separate State for the North within the United Kingdom. George V had a hand in the moves for peace when he opened the Northern Ireland Parliament on June 22, 1921, with a surprisingly sympathetic and eloquent "prayer" for peace in Ireland. But that successful launching pad for peace was double-edged. Peace now would be a peace of partition in Ireland, and not even de Valera seemed to see its real significance.

On that same day in June de Valera was arrested by accident, but within a few hours, as

During the Anglo-Irish War—from January 1919 to July 1921 when the Truce was declared—many atrocities were enacted by British forces, as for example, the farmyard carnage in West Cork, recorded in a photograph album of a British officer. The British established an auxiliary force, the so-called Black-and-Tans, to replace the almost non-existent Royal Irish Constabulary. A unit (below) of Tans stationed at Union Quay, Cork.

De Valera (arrowed) was swept off his feet by enthusiastic supporters outside the Mansion House in Dublin during the discussion to settle the Truce arrangements with the British in July, 1921.

the Lloyd George plan for settlement developed, he was removed to comfortable officers' quarters in Portobello where, it is recorded, "he just sat down and read a book on war by General Foch". The next day he was released and on June 25 he received the historic letter from Lloyd George proposing a conference between himself, de Valera and Sir James Craig. From his meetings with Southern Unionists, however, came a proposal for a Truce between the armed forces of the Republic and of Britain. The Truce came into operation on July 11, 1921. It was indeed a great day for Ireland. England had been forced to seek peace. It was a victory of which de Valera was the chief architect.

On July 12, 1921, an appropriate day, de Valera was on his way to London to open negotiations with Lloyd George about the future of Ireland. He was accompanied by Griffith, Stack, Barton, Plunkett and Erskine Childers, as advisers, but not as negotiators. Two days later Lloyd George and de Valera began their historic talks. At their meeting de Valera suggested that the words Irish Republic could best be translated as "Saorstát na hEireann". Lloyd George thought the name apt.

The Treaty and Civil War

It is of interest, as the London talks opened, to review de Valera's policy on Irish unity as his political experience from 1917 to 1921 widened his vision. In retrospect it could be seen that the attitude to that issue may have been the achilles heel of Ireland's Republicans.

One of his first statements on the North on the occasion of the Clare election in 1917 was uncompromising. It said: "Let Ulster Unionists recognise the Sinn Féin position which has behind it justice and right. It is supported by nine-tenths of the Irish people and if those Unionists do not come in on our side, they will have to go under. Ulster is entitled to justice and she will have it, but she should not be petted and the interests of the majority sacrificed to her. Give Unionists a just and full share of representation, but no more than their just share."

Later in the spring of 1918 when Sinn Féin lost three by-elections, de Valera wrote: "I say that Sinn Féin is the only power to deal with the Orangeman. Let the North fall back on their fortress of the two races, their fortress of partition—that has no terrors for us. Let them fall back on it, they will find it a Metz (the French fortress). It is after all only an old fortress of crumbled masonry—held together with a plaster of fiction."

In May 1921 his rejection of Sir James Craig's offer of dominion status was another sign of a die-hard attitude and yet his use of the machinery of the Partition general election of May 1921 was interpreted as a form of acceptance of Partition. Yet in August, 1921, his statement in the Dáil that Ulster must not be subjected to Republican force, and arguing county option was that of a man who completely understood the Northern situation. That understanding, however, seemed to be a contradiction of a statement he made to me in 1970 after an article on Erskine Childers had appeared in The Irish Times. He said: "Erskine Childers knew far more about the North than I did. I always thought that it was caused by the leaders of the Covenanters and a few British Tories. Childers knew it went far deeper than that. I didn't." It was a courageous statement after 50 years, but also tragic in that it seemed to be the mind of a man who was at the centre of the Partition problem for more than 50 years. And yet, around the same time in 1970, he was able to say to me that "at heart the Northern Protestant is an Irishman and would declare so if given a fair opportunity."

The Northern State

The establishment of that Northern State in June 1921, however, though not the beginning of Partition—that had existed in people's minds for at least a century—was Partition institutionalised. Now the Loyalists had their own State, with all the resources for organisation and security, a State that could mobilise the entire Protestant community against absorption into Southern Ireland. No wonder Lloyd George exploited King George's peaceful approach, for now, with the North established, he could well afford to make peace with the South. Republican optimism, however, hid the grim reality that Ireland was divided not alone in outlook but in the physical presence of a Northern Parliament and Government.

That was the reality as de Valera left Dublin on July 12, 1921, to meet Lloyd George at Downing Street for the first talks on the future of Ireland. The Prime Minister's original invitation had urged a meeting between himself, de Valera and Sir James Craig, and a similar invitation had been sent to Craig addressed to him as "Premier of Northern Ireland". De Valera, however, saw the trap and sought meetings with "the political minority in this country". Correspondence continued after the Truce was declared between the two armies, and a meeting was arranged to discuss "the basis on which to achieve the object desired."

The two leaders met on July 14, 15, 18 and 21, but proposals from Britain were

Republican members elected to the First Dáil in 1919

Front row: L. Ginnell, M. Collins, C. Brugha, A. Griffith, E. de Valera, Count George Plunkett, E. MacNeill, W. Cosgrave, E. Blythe.

Second row: P. Malony, T. MacSwiney, D. Mulcahy, J. Doherty, J. O'Mahony, J. Dolan, J. McGuinness, P. O'Keeffe, M. Staines, J. McGrath, Dr. Cusack, L. De Roiste, W. Colivet, Father Michael O'Flanagan.

Third row: P. Ward, A. McCabe, D. FitzGerald, J. Sweeney, Dr. Hayes, C. Collins, P. O Maille, J. O'Mara, B. O'Higgins, J. Burke, K. O'Higgins.

Fourth row: J. McDonagh, J. McEntee.

Fifth row: P. Beasley, R. Barton, P. Galligan.

Sixth row: P. Shanahan, S. Etchingham.

The first Irish delegation to London, July 12, 1921:
R. C. Barton, de Valera, Count George Plunkett,
Arthur Griffith and Erskine Childers.

rejected by de Valera and later by his Government and the Dáil. Britain's offer invited Ireland to set up a dominion state as part of the British Empire, which contained so many millions of Irish, but conditions were that Ireland should co-operate in defence matters, the British Navy would control the seas around Ireland, and Ireland would afford all facilities which Britain needed in Irish ports, etc. There were to be no protective duties on either side. But it accepted that the Northern State would remain separate unless the people of the North deemed otherwise.

De Valera's rejection stated that the defence conditions would make Ireland a helpless "dependency". On unity de Valera said they would be prepared to enter into *"a treaty of free association with the British Commonwealth group, had we an assurance that the entry of the Irish nation as a whole into such association would secure for it the allegiance of the present dissenting minority, to meet whose sentiment alone, this step should be contemplated."*

Talk of reconciliation
De Valera insisted that in regard to the national minority the Irish people alone must be the means of resolving that. *"If your Government*

stands aside we can effect a complete reconciliation." The Irish people could not admit the right of Britain to "mutilate our country".

It is of some interest that de Valera—guarding his flanks—addressed the T.U.C. in Dublin and the President of the T.U.C. gave him backing in his quest for freedom.

One cannot but admire the superb diplomacy which characterised all of the many letters which de Valera sent to Lloyd George from July to the end of September. Ultimately a conference was arranged for October 11. The magic words which made that possible were contained in Lloyd George's later letters: "A conference where we can meet your delegates as spokesmen of the people whom you represent with a view to ascertaining how the association of Ireland with the community of nations known as the British Empire may best be reconciled with Irish national aspirations."

Those Treaty negotiations began on October 11, 1921, and went on to December 6 when the outlines of the new Treaty were signed, a Treaty which later led to the Civil War. It would be useful to outline de Valera's own views given to this writer years later about that period. He looked upon the Truce first with a lot of pessimism. He thought peace was impossible, but the Truce would give the Army a chance of rest and re-grouping and re-equipping, and give the people a respite from their hardships, but he believed that fighting inevitably would have to be resumed. When, therefore, one Minister urged in Cabinet that the Army should be disbanded he strongly resisted the proposal, and was warmly supported by Ernest Blythe, who later opposed de Valera on the Treaty. They seemed to envisage a situation that where the other side might win an election, "we did not want to be helpless".

It was when he received Lloyd George's letter of September 7 with that phrase about Ireland's aspirations and association with the British Empire, that he saw, at last, a hope of peace. That phrase "association" stuck in his mind and he initiated a discussion on it in the Cabinet, but no progress could be made. "One morning in September," he told me, "I was tying my boot-laces when the word 'external' came into my mind. 'That's it,' I said, 'that's it, external association with the British Empire'. I then could go to the Cabinet with my mind

De Valera arriving at Downing Street for his meeting with Lloyd George.

clear. Later they all saw the significance of the word 'external' and accepted it. Only Eoin MacNeill quarrelled a bit with it, saying 'I hope it won't mean anything more than external association!' I replied: 'It will not' and he accepted that." And thus was the way opened to the historic negotiations.

De Valera also recalled that before meeting the Cabinet he wrote a note to Cathal Brugha asking him to write down his definition of external association. Brugha did this and de Valera said (in June 1968) he had kept that letter ever since. (He opened his drawer there and then, took out the letter and handed it to me. It showed that de Valera and Brugha were at one in their definition of a Republic in voluntary association with the group of nations known as the British Empire or Commonwealth.)

The signing in London

But that device failed to win either the Irish or the British, and on December 6, 1921, Griffith,

The men who signed the Treaty: Griffith, Duggan, Barton and Gavan Duffy. Collins travelled separately to the negotiations in London.

Collins, Barton, Duffy and Duggan signed the Heads of a Treaty between Ireland and Great Britain. Lloyd George had demonstrated that the alternative to signing would have been "immediate war", but de Valera bitterly opposed the Treaty. His objections were that it insisted on Ireland's allegiance to the Crown, the link with the Empire, the right of British occupation for defence purposes, and was to set up an Irish Free State, not an Irish Republic; a Governor-General would act for the King of England. One of the strongest arguments for the signing, however, was that it had been forced on the plenipotentiaries under threat. Barton did say later that Collins also had threatened him. He told him that if his (Barton's) refusal to sign the Treaty resulted in a new war in Ireland then *"You Barton will swing from a lamp-post in Dublin."*

Strangely, while the question of national unity was the major issue of the Treaty negotiations, it was not so in the Dáil debates: both those who were pro-Treaty and those against, all assumed that the Boundary Commission which the Treaty set up, would resolve that problem.

At a Cabinet meeting in Dublin on December 7 without the Cabinet signatories who were still in London, de Valera announced his rejection and only the pleas of W. T. Cosgrave persuaded him not to dismiss Collins, Griffith and Barton. The next day, the full Cabinet met and split. Griffith, Collins, Barton and W. T. Cosgrave accepted the Treaty, while de Valera, Cathal Brugha and Austin Stack rejected. All hope of some form of compromise between the leaders seemed impossible, and de Valera announced publicly that night that the Cabinet had been divided and that he would not recommend the Treaty to the Dáil or the people; the Dáil would decide.

The Dáil after a debate lasting several weeks accepted the Treaty by 64 to 57 votes. On January 10 a Dáil Executive under Griffith was elected; de Valera was defeated as President only by two votes.

Griffith was to become President in his place. Even those who had voted for the Treaty still wished de Valera to be President. It was a narrow shave for the Treaty, but de Valera and his supporters walked out as Griffith was nominated as President.

On January 14 a meeting described as the Parliament of Southern Ireland, but really a meeting of the Pro-Treaty Deputies, elected a Provisional Government which was headed by Michael Collins, as Chairman or Premier, and his task was to establish the Irish Free State, Saorstát na h-Eireann. Two days later the British Army, including the Black-and-Tans, and the Auxiliaries, another sinister force, began to leave Ireland. Collins took possession of Dublin Castle as British troops left Ireland after 750 years. In their place came Irish Volunteers. The Royal Irish Constabulary was disbanded and the organisation began of a new police force—the Civic Guard. Collins and Mulcahy began the building of a professional Army. Already, however, there were signs of the formation of another army—the anti-Treaty I.R.A. In the Dáil, at the same time, de Valera formed a new party, Cumann na Poblachta. He declared that the 57 deputies who had voted against the Treaty would act as an ordinary Opposition. It was the first parliamentary opposition since the Dáil was established in January 1919.

Arthur Griffith, elected President by a two-vote majority over de Valera.

Carnage of civil war

Six months later began the Civil War between the Treaty and anti-Treaty I.R.A. and before it ended almost 800 had died and thousands were maimed.

Thus the great Sinn Féin movement which had forced Britain to call a halt, was destroyed. For years afterwards de Valera was accused as the sole cause of the Civil War. His refusal to be one of the plenipotentiaries himself was a main criticism; another was that his fiery speeches, and warnings that "brothers would fight against brothers" to abolish the Treaty, had incited civil war. His own defence has been that had Griffith not given his express undertaking to refer proposals to the Dáil before signing, he would have gone himself. Indeed, he told me: *"I had made up my mind to go to that last meeting with Lloyd George until Griffith gave his undertaking."*

He remained at home so that, in the event of any moderation of terms to bring in the North he would be able to keep the extreme wing united with Sinn Féin and rally the people in support of a settlement. Had the Treaty been put to the Dáil before rejection, he said, Lloyd George would not have declared war. *"He once told me that he could put enough troops into Ireland for every man, woman and child. I had replied, 'yes, but you will have to keep them there which is another thing, and you will have to get the support of your own people.' And so I stayed at home."*

Had the Dáil rejected the Treaty he was confident he would have been able to secure advances himself on the basis of the Document No. 2 which, in effect, would have been the

45

Cartoon commentary
—from the March,
April and May issues
of *Dublin Opinion*
in 1922

Mayflowers

St. Peter: *In you go.*

Arthur: *Righto, it'll be heavenly.*

Michael: *I'm a bit doubtful, but I'll try it
for a while.*

Eamon: *I'll go below; it may be easier
to get out.*

M-m-must we part?

position reached in 1938, external association of a 26-county Ireland with Britain. Had he failed with Lloyd George he would have put it to the British people, he said. He also claimed that Collins's influence with the I.R.B. was the decisive factor in securing a majority in the Dáil for the Treaty. The Dáil members of the I.R.B. had been told of the I.R.B. approval of the Treaty though they were given a free hand in the vote on it. But a majority of the H.Q. Staff of the I.R.A. under Collins accepted the Treaty and founded the new Provisional Government's national army. An interesting point de Valera made to me was that he would have included the famous Mary MacSwiney in the team of pleni-potentiaries, but that Collins and Griffith were, in principle, against the inclusion of women.

A possible reason for de Valera's manoeuvring at that time could have been that he feared Collins as a potential rival. His view was that Collins might differ with him on a Treaty which would be less than the Republic and would then seek to be leader of a separate Republican Party. But in fact de Valera knew long before December 1921 that Collins would accept the Crown.

Stripped of power

De Valera was confident too that had the vote been taken before Christmas 1921 the Treaty would have been rejected. In the interval to January the press and the Church campaigned strongly for acceptance, and this was decisive in changing the minds of some deputies.

By January 16, 1922, de Valera had been stripped of all his power as President and Prime Minister, his power over Sinn Féin severely damaged and his authority over the Army dissipated. Griffith now was President, Collins was Head of the Provisional Government, and Mulcahy Minister for Defence of the pro-Treaty section of the Army. Liam Lynch was the Chief of Staff of the anti-Treaty I.R.A. De Valera, apart from his name and prestige as President of Sinn Féin, was now merely leader of Cumann na Poblachta Dáil Eireann still existed, but the real authority was the Provisional Government headed by Collins. The anti-Treaty I.R.A. declared its independence of any political party, even de Valera's or Brugha's, though both still remained friendly with Liam Lynch, Liam Mellows and other I.R.A. leaders. Their only authority now was their own executive led by Lynch.

Efforts for peace by Sinn Féin, not yet disrupted, continued and produced, as the Civil War drew ever nearer, the famous Collins-de Valera Pact for the 1922 Election. It envisaged a coalition Government of Pro- and Anti-Treaty parties and armies, and de Valera, in denying his responsibility for civil war, told me later: *"During the Pact Election I never said a word for or against the Treaty. I travelled to Pact meetings with Deputy Seán Hales and others who supported the Treaty, but Collins later broke that Pact, and then went on to stage a coup d'etat when he used the Army to take over*

De Valera speaking on behalf of the Republican party during the 'pact' election campaign in June 1922.

47

The Custom House in Dublin, repository of many of the country's vital records, was attacked by the Irish Republican Army in May, 1921: almost everything was destroyed. The action was deemed politically important as a means to impede the British administration.

power." De Valera also believed that Collins was under pressure from Churchill; A. J. P. Taylor, British historian, concurs.

There were, however, other factors. On June 18, two days after the general election, in which the pro-Treaty Parties won an overwhelming majority, Rory O'Connor, Liam Mellows, Joe McKelvey and others broke with the Lynch section of the I.R.A. when O'Connor's section was defeated narrowly on a motion at an I.R.A. Convention that war should be resumed immediately by the I.R.A. against the British.

Anti-Treatyites sundered

O'Connor and his forces then occupied the Four Courts enforcing the exclusion of the Lynch section which had been with them when they occupied the law offices on April 14,

1922. They appointed Joe McKelvey as the new Chief-of-Staff and a new army Executive and refused entry to Lynch, Brugha and their men: even de Valera was locked out. At the crisis Convention, O'Connor's men denied Brugha the right to speak and were reluctant to let Mellows speak, because both were "politicians". The split had caused a new division. Now even the anti-Treaty I.R.A. was split, so there were three armies, three chiefs-of-staff, three army executives, perhaps even three governments, apart from the British, the Northern Ireland Government and the Government elected by the Dáil—a total of six Governments. It certainly was a civil war situation. De Valera sought to plead with the irreconcilables, but was helpless.

The existence of the new split was known, of course, to Collins and Mulcahy and could have been the decisive reason for the Civil War. On June 26, four days after the assassination of Sir Henry Wilson in London, for which de Valera believed Collins responsible, Ernie O'Malley and Seán MacBride, acting on their own, it appears, arrested Ginger O'Connell, deputy chief of the Provisional Government Army, while he was visiting his girl-friend. Collins, believing the Four Courts I.R.A. to be only a section of the I.R.A. at war with Liam Lynch, urged the Provisional Government to attack the building, and this was agreed. The Government already felt a new and greater authority from its election victory. But information was incomplete; that very day the Lynch and O'Connor wings at a conference reached agreement for a new convention and so the Government Army attack on the Four Courts re-united the I.R.A. The Civil War had begun. Even the politicians like de Valera, Brugha, MacEntee, Jim Ryan and many others felt that the attack was a crime and re-joined their units. De Valera described the I.R.A. as "the last and bravest of our nation" adding his moral strength to them and their cause.

De Valera later explained to me his position: "I joined as a private soldier, but I went to the Hamman Hotel and urged the I.R.A. leadership there to try and make peace. I got Father Albert to go to Collins, but when he did see him, Collins's reply was 'They must first lay down their arms.' Collins then prevented the Dáil (after the 1922 election) from meeting on July 1st as laid down by the official Proclamation and thus was lost all chance of peace." De Valera still believed that a coalition government could have been formed after the election and even after the Four Courts had been attacked.

And so the Civil War went on with all its tragedy, with the deaths of Griffith, Brugha, Harry Boland, Collins, Erskine Childers and Liam Lynch. In the early spring of 1923, however, de Valera, who in September 1922 had again been accepted by the I.R.A., made even stronger efforts to get the Lynch I.R.A. to end hostilities. "It was difficult to talk to them" he recalled for me. "Liam Lynch seemed to rely on promises made to him that guns could be

August 17, 1922: The final step in the transfer of Dublin Castle to the Irish Free State was the hand-over by the Royal Irish Constabulary to the newly-formed Civic Guard police force. The first detachment entered the Castle yard led by the Commissioner, Mr. M. Staines, T.D., and Chief Superintendent M. McCarthy.

The shelling of the Four Courts by Provisional
Government troops sparked off the
Civil War in June, 1922.

Removing the elderly to safety
during the shelling in central Dublin.

brought to them 'on horse-back'. I told him that no guns were coming but he was resolved to fight on. On his death I got Frank Aiken, who was then Chief-of-Staff, to persuade the I.R.A. to 'dump arms' and declare a cease-fire." He went on: "If there is any man in Ireland who deserves the highest tribute of the Irish people, it is Frank Aiken. In the Civil War situation he fought for peace all the time."

Influence of Collins

Now that de Valera is dead, can that Civil War issue be looked at more dispassionately? Certainly after it, Republican Ireland, and its leader, de Valera, was well and truly battered, scattered and destroyed. What a debacle after such hopes of triumph. It certainly was a descent for de Valera from the high peak of the Truce of 1921 to the despairing valley of brother in war against brother. It seemed the end of the road for the man who had seen such glory.

There were, of course, many factors underlying the outbreak of Civil War. No one factor caused it, and no one leader or person. Peadar O'Donnell, in his forthright defence of de Valera says that Collins had far more influence on the I.R.A. than de Valera, and yet he was unable to persuade the hard men to lay down their guns.

Were the causes in the political arena? Sinn Féin, of course, consisted of three main sections, the Volunteers led mainly by de Valera on the political side, the I.R.B. led by Collins with his enormous influence over the I.R.A., and the old Sinn Féin led by Griffith. The Treaty vote was decided perhaps by the strange combination of the extreme conservative group, Sinn Féin, and the apparently extreme left (militarily) the I.R.B., against the centre, led by de Valera. That combination of the right and the left proved to be invincible. The I.R.B. had voted overwhelmingly in conference and in the Supreme Council for the Treaty. That was a powerful influence. Then there had been the strong endorsement of the Treaty by the 1922 general election, giving a new authority to Collins, while the assassination of Wilson brought pressure from London. But the strongest factor of all could have been that split in the anti-Treaty I.R.A. and its seizure of the Four Courts. Again, the business interests and the Churches and the trade unions were strongly for the Treaty.

Demolishing a central Dublin block in the aftermath of the Civil War.

It has been said with some justice that de Valera's speeches against the Treaty, about "Irishmen wading through the blood of Irishmen" were "words that kill" but de Valera claims that those extracts of his speeches were taken from context, that they were warnings of the dangers ahead, not incitement. But young men, armed, and with patriotism deep in them from the "Four Glorious Years" were easily stimulated to action. An armed nation divided adds up to civil war.

Perhaps the grim fact is that de Valera's political leadership, so superb in those earlier four years, failed within an ace of success. That postponement of the Debate in December 1921 was an important factor, and the final vote, it must be remembered, caused his defeat by the tiny margin of seven votes. Even later, on the vote for re-election as President he lost by only two votes. All divisions were total: there was no compromise.

Ernest Blythe claims there had been a civil war situation since February 1922, when an armed clash between the two armies had been only barely averted in Limerick by Mulcahy. W. T. Cosgrave did admit in the Dáil on December 6, 1922 that a pact had existed but that the I.R.A. threat to resume immediately the fight against the British forces was too deadly serious to postpone the Four Courts attack. Because of the apparent isolation of the Four Courts' I.R.A. the Government expected the engagement to last but a few hours.

De Valera, who had been
elected to the Six County
Parliament as the Sinn Féin
member for South Down in 1921,
was arrested by the Royal Ulster
Constabulary when he visited
Newry in 1924. An order forbade
his entry into the North. Later,
visiting Derry, he was again
arrested and imprisoned for a
month in Belfast.

Playing chess with Austin Stack
in Arbour Hill barracks after his
arrest in Ennis in 1923. The two
prisoners, like thousands of other
republicans, had been on the run
from the Free State forces
following the end of the Civil
War.

The founding of Fianna Fáil

De Valera sometimes, surprisingly, expressed his opinion to this writer that "the Civil War was not *wholly* negative", but he never elaborated on its positive features. It could be that it was the beginning of new Ireland's parliamentary-democracy, from the parties formed on that issue, or, perhaps, that the Civil War kept the national flame alive for a further surge forward. Certainly when one surveyed the national scene after the Civil War something new clearly was needed. Young or old Republicans viewing the scene would have been dismayed that, after the "Four Glorious Years" and all the sacrifices, Ireland now was ruled by Cumann na nGael, the most conservative wing in the South in those days, with Tim Healy, the former arch-enemy of Parnell, now Governor-General, and by the Unionist Party in the North. The Rising, the First and Second Dáil, and all that, had been in vain. By August 1923, de Valera and 12,000 of his followers were in jail.

That period of total defeat—from October 1922 to August 1923—however, when de Valera was harassed, humiliated, "on the run" for his life, as told by historians and biographers, reveals the man's extraordinary political qualities, and powers of resilience. Even in the darkest hour of those dark days, he did not give up hope or stop working. Even as Erskine Childers, and later, Mellows, and his comrades were being executed, he was meeting men like Paddy Ruttledge, and others, telling them that they must now get down to building the political organisation, Sinn Féin. "No matter what way the war ends, there will have to be a political solution." He had noticed that Cosgrave and the others had not tried to revive Sinn Féin of which he was still nominally, at least, President and so the call went out: *"Build Sinn Féin."*

Changed situation

Since the establishment of the new State in December 1922, his whole analysis of the political situation had changed. The existence of an Irish State with all its financial and executive resources had created an entirely new situation.

His thinking may have dated even from January 16, 1922, after his Dáil defeat and the appointment of a Provisional Government under Collins. Whatever chance military force had had against the British, such force had no chance against an Irish State, particularly when the people of the State had given a majority vote to the Government. The fight back had to be political. There was no other way. Reversing Clausewicz, he decided *"Politics is war by other means".*

Getting a political party revived in the circumstances of civil war was many times more difficult than establishing Sinn Féin in 1917 when enthusiasm was everywhere. But in 1922–3 Sinn Féin was revived even in the few months before the general election of August 1923, and that election must have been a tonic. Sinn Féin received 44 seats, a gain of eight, and 286,000 first preference votes against Cumann na nGael's 63 seats, a gain of five on 1922, and about 415,000 first preferences. De Valera in East Clare received 17,700 votes against 8,190 for his opponent, Eoin MacNeill. It was an extraordinary recovery.

At an East Clare election meeting de Valera had been nearly assassinated. The attempt sprang from the bitterness of the time. Henry Harrison, Parnell's famous secretary has told that after the Civil War began, he had been asked by a Government Minister to join a special squad to round up the most dangerous men and to quell riots. He was asked specially to arrest de Valera, but was told that he need not be too particular about whether he was alive or not. Harrison ignored that advice, and became a close associate of de Valera later. But a group of Free State Army officers had planned to shoot him in Ennis in August, 1923, and had actually selected a marksman. At the last moment, however, as the late Ernest Blythe related, the marksman was changed, and the second choice missed his target. Years later the first marksman lamented his removal from the assassination attempt.

The Free State Executive Council in October, 1922: Major-General Joseph McGrath, Hugh Kennedy William Cosgrave, Ernest Blythe, Kevin O'Higgins and J. J. Walsh.

Obstacle of the Oath

De Valera, of course, was arrested, but on his release in July 1924 he began to implement his new thinking. Now minds were to be turned towards the Dáil, and the possibility of joining in that assembly. It was an assembly of the people, whatever Republicans thought of it. But first the Oath had to be removed. That was now the only obstacle to the progress of the nation. In July 1924, as President of Sinn Féin and President of the I.R.A. and a member of the Army Council with Frank Aiken and, later Seán Lemass, he sought to turn the Army into political channels. The Army had agreed that de Valera's Government was the controlling body on national matters, but in 1925 when an Army Convention heard the idea of abolishing the Oath and entering the Dáil, the delegates revolted, and led the Army away from de Valera and his illegal Government, and Sinn Féin. Again the anti-Treaty Republicans were to split.

Almost as that split occurred, however, there was the news that the Boundary Commission, which had been set up under the Treaty and which was expected to give extra territory to the Free State, had had its report nullified by an agreement between the Free State Government and the British. The agreement accepted the existing Border and also had agreed to delete the Treaty arrangement to establish a Council of Ireland. The news caused wide disappointment and strong protests among Republicans. Now Partition was being accepted and recognised by the Free State Government and at once de Valera recognised it as the one issue that would arouse the greatest interest.

As the shrewdest of politicians, now with hopes of power growing as four by-elections fell to him, Mr. de Valera saw his party, Sinn Féin, as the only serious contender for the post of leader of a nation determined to end Partition. A meeting of all Sinn Féin Deputies ended in a statement in which de Valera said: "We may have to bow our heads for a time to enforced Partition by a foreign power, but that Partition can never have the sanction of our consent.. . . If this generation should be base enough to give the Northern Counties away, the right to win them back remains unimpaired for those to whom the future will bring the opportunity."

With the Border as the midwife new developments followed quickly. The Labour Party strongly urged de Valera to enter the Dáil and defeat the Partition Bill but he refused, and instead, after the split with the I.R.A., decided to put his whole new policy on the Oath and the

54

Michael Collins bearing the coffin of Arthur Griffith, who died in August 1922, flanked by Michael Hayes, Speaker of the Third Dáil, and J. J. Walsh, Minister for Posts and Telegraphs. Collins, who was Chief of Staff of the Free State forces, was killed in an ambush at Béal na Bláth, Co. Cork, the same month.

Dáil before a Sinn Féin ard-fheis in March 1926. By this time Sinn Féin had recovered much of its old strength and had held successful ard-fheiseanna in 1923, 1924 and 1925.

De Valera proposed a motion at that 1926 ard-fheis that Sinn Féin should concentrate all its efforts to secure the abolition of the Oath and then enter the Dáil as an assembly of Ireland's elected representatives. But the motion was defeated by 223 votes to 218, though the movers of the rejection, Father O'Flanagan and Mary MacSwiney later moved a proposal expressing the admiration of the ard-fheis for de Valera and his work for Ireland. In that debate one delegate described the President as the "greatest Irishman of a century", and the motion was carried unanimously. Because, however, several delegates had declared they would leave if de

Valera's motion had been carried, he decided to resign from Sinn Féin: *"A split was inevitable either way."*

Recalling that day he told me that as he and the late Seán Lemass *"walked away from the hall, I told him 'it looks as if that is the end for me, Seán. I'm chucking politics altogether'."* Lemass retorted *"but you can't leave us now, Dev. We must go on."* After further argument he agreed.

The early organisation

A few days later in de Valera's home in Serpentine Avenue, Sandymount, Dublin, he met Seán T. O'Kelly, Seán Lemass, Seán MacEntee, Paddy Ruttledge, Frank Aiken, Jim Ryan and Gerry Boland and within little more than a month, after new efforts to win agreement with

HIS MASTER'S VOICE

FIANNA FÁIL

MAKE YOUR VOICE HEARD
BY VOTING FOR
CUMANN NA nGAEDHEAL

*Anti-Dev campaign . . . a poster used by the
Government party in the 1927 election.*

Sinn Féin failed, there began the formation of a
new organisation, the third formed by de Valera
since the first Sinn Féin of 1917. By April 13
the first branches were being organised as he
toured the country in a battered and aged car.
On May 16, 1926 Fianna Fáil was launched at
an overflow meeting in the La Scala, Dublin,
beside the G.P.O. Less than six months later
more than 500 delegates attended the first
ard-fheis—the fourth anniversary of the death
of Erskine Childers.

Argument over name
De Valera and Lemass had quite an argument
about whether the name should be Fianna Fáil
or the Republican Party; they compromised by
naming it Fianna Fáil with the "Republican

Party" in brackets. *"Fianna Fáil"*, de Valera
later explained, *"had been the original name of
the Irish Volunteers and brought back the
Easter Week tradition, giving a proper continuity to Fianna Fáil. Fianna Fáil was built on
the same military, hierarchical principles as the
Volunteers and Sinn Féin, and its members were
'citizen soldiers'."* De Valera also said that
Fianna Fáil had the advantage that the name
could not be translated; perhaps "Citizen
Soldiers" is a good translation.

At the La Scala meeting he showed real
political skill when he reduced the whole
complex political situation of that time to the
single issue of the Oath. If that were abolished
then the new party, which already had 44
(former Sinn Féin) deputies, could make a bid
for power, securing all the resources of the
State to accomplish their national and social
aims. These were, he declared: 1. Political
independence of a United Ireland as a Republic;
2. Restoration of the language and national
culture; 3. Development of a social system in
which, as far as possible equal opportunity
will be afforded to every Irish citizen to live a
noble and useful, Christian life; distribution of
land to get the greatest possible number of Irish
families rooted in the soil; making Ireland an
economic unit with a proper balance between
agricultural and other essential industries.

In his speeches at the La Scala, and elsewhere
the great issue was the abolition of the Oath and
then, forward to the United Republic, but the
workers in the cities and towns were wooed
also with industrial development, new social
welfare, health insurance, widows and orphans'
pensions, family allowances, and with the odd
quote from Connolly such as *"Ireland as distinct
from its people means nothing to me."* He did
not add those other words: *"And the man or
woman who believe themselves to be patriots
and who can look upon the poverty and misery
in their native land without crying out to end it,
is a fraud and a liar in his heart."* Later he made
this important statement which won him many
supporters: *"It may be that under the present
system we cannot do the full work we would
like to do, but we will try. If I try within the
system as it stands, and fail, then I will try to go
ahead outside the system and I will go to the
country and ask them to support me to go
outside the system."*

De Valera and supporters at the foundation meeting of Fianna Fáil in 1926.

Few can criticise de Valera in founding Fianna Fáil. Both Sinn Féin and the I.R.A. had reached a dead end. Whatever he might say publicly, privately he pleaded with the I.R.A. that physical force to change the Treaty or to end Partition was useless, and would lead again to civil war. With him into Fianna Fáil he took great figures like Countess Markievicz, Mrs. Pearse, Miss Margaret Pearse, Mrs. Tom Clarke, Paddy Ruttledge, Frank Aiken, Oscar Traynor, Tom Derrig, Seán Moylan and the great majority of a whole generation of militant Republicans. It was an achievement that added, if it did not create, the Irish parliamentary system as we know it today. The achievement of creating such a powerful organisation in the apathy and despair of 1925–26 can hardly ever be appreciated.

Now, de Valera was no longer the national revolutionary of 1917: he was the leader of an opposition party and as such his *raison d'etre* was to gain power. The party grew steadily and within about three months of its first ard-fheis it won 44 seats in the Dáil in June, 1927. The decision to enter the Dáil was a tortuous one because he had to reconcile his firmest declarations against taking the Oath of Allegiance by convincing himself that it was a mere formula. He quoted R. M. Smyllie as telling him that Cosgrave was shocked when he told him: "*Dev is going in.*"

'I took no Oath'

"*I knew*", he recalled later "*that even Cosgrave's men did not like the Oath and that it was now taken in a back-room at Leinster House. All people had to do was to sign a book. There was no formal or solemn declaration. The Clerk of the Dáil, Colm O Murchada, told me when we entered Leinster House, 'all I want is your signature in the book there.' I put the Bible away and then signed my name as I would if I were signing an autograph. I took no Oath,*" he told me.

He recalled that day of the Oath. "*I sat down in my seat as Leader of the Opposition and I* heard the Ceann Comhairle read out the names of those who had 'fulfilled the Article of the Constitution . . . .' I half-stood up in my seat to protest at this interpretation, but then I said to myself 'sit down you fool, that's his interpretation, not yours. Let them have it that way.' And so I sat down and said nothing." He said that he had had confirmation from a theologian, Canon Watters, later, that he had not taken an oath.

On the first day in the Dáil he almost toppled the Government through a coalition voting arrangement with the Labour Party, the National League, Independents and others, but the famous Mayor Jinks of Sligo, by abstaining saved the day for the Government. Within six weeks or so, however, Fianna Fáil secured 57 seats, and almost 412,000 votes in the general election that was then called, only five seats less than Cosgrave obtained, but he had however, gained 15 extra seats, and so was safe for another five years. De Valera's policy of the taking the oath and entering the Dáil had been overwhelmingly endorsed by his supporters in that election. Fianna Fáil grew as more republicans joined.

Votes now the new battalions

In his new role as Leader of the Parliamentary Opposition he was also a complete success. Votes were now the new battalions, the new means to power. At a time when he had hardly a single supporter among the bishops or the senior clergy he began to work to win Catholic Church support. The radical who had stood up to clericalism, could be heard now protesting against the appointment of a Protestant girl as the librarian in Mayo, or of a Protestant doctor elsewhere. And the Government Minister, General Mulcahy, supported the appointments. De Valera supported Seán T. O'Kelly when he urged that prayers should be said before the Dáil debates began each day and that the Dáil should not meet on holy days. In each case the Cumann na nGael Government opposed the motions. He kept his lines open with the I.R.A. by his speeches that the State was illegitimate, that it had been won by a coup d'etat, and that the I.R.A. had a logical link with the early Sinn Féin or by opposing repressive security measures. Lemass, also

secured Republican support when he declared Fianna Fáil to be a "slightly constitutional party", prepared to try politics but prepared also to try tougher methods, if they did not succeed. The farmers also had to be won over and this was tried by the policy of retaining the Land Annuities, or by new investment for tillage, and for protection against foreign foods.

Businessmen, Catholic and Protestant, would not have been too alarmed about his references to James Connolly and "going outside the system". They had noted the familiar qualifications and many of them would have recalled the conservative social character of the First and Second Dáil. Some of them, however, might have been concerned of new feelings in the North at the de Valera opening of the new drive on partition. Fianna Fáil was now the party of United Ireland and it did not neglect to blame Britain for partition.

As the great world economic crisis of 1929 and the early Thirties hit Ireland and with growing unemployment and poverty and sometimes real starvation, the Cosgrave Government was unable to meet the burden and sought to meet unrest with more repressive laws. The I.R.A. was becoming more aggressive and de Valera was prominent in opposing the resulting repression. He might have known that the I.R.A., then quite a powerful organisation, would be useful during the expected general election in early 1932. So as de Valera's great activities expanded so did the I.R.A.

And now, after almost 20 years of national activity of some kind, from Easter Week, to death sentence, jail, national leadership, civil war, and again jail, de Valera in his fiftieth year in 1931, was ready for power. During his four years in Opposition he had shown himself to be the country's leading politician. As Cosgrave called the general election for February, 1932, de Valera's manifesto was radical and yet cautious. The Oath must go; Land Annuities be retained; but the Republic was not mentioned. Indeed, there was a guarantee that nothing drastic would be done without the consent of the people, protection would be applied to industry and agriculture, and social welfare would be extended. De Valera denied that his party was Communist, but the campaign by the Church against him was very tough.

BARRIER OF THE OATH:
Twice in the summer of
1927 de Valera and his
colleagues attempted to
enter the Dáil for the first
time as Fianna Fáil
deputies. The group (right)
of Seán Lemass, de Valera,
Seán T. O'Kelly,
P. J. Ruttledge and Seán
MacEntee withdrew on
June 23 after refusing to
take the Oath of Allegiance
to the King of England.
On August 11 de Valera,
flanked by Ruttledge, Gerry
Boland and Countess
Markievicz and other
deputies (below), returned
to Leinster House and
signed their names before
the Clerk of the House.
They did not swear on the
Bible.

The return to power

Yet he won a great victory, securing more than 566,000 votes, or nearly 120,000 more than Cumann na nGael, with 72 seats against 57. He had very nearly doubled his vote since March, 1927. With the support of the seven Labour deputies, headed by William Norton, he became President of the Government of the very Free State he had fought against. In spite of fears of army resistance, the victors in the Civil War handed over power peacefully to the defeated side. Democracy had certainly come to Ireland. De Valera had not even to be appointed officially by the Governor-General, James MacNeill, who actually called after the election to his room in Leinster House, simply saying "May I congratulate you, Mr. de Valera". The appointment was made and a revolution was effected by a handshake.

Now he had supreme power; he was in control of all the resources and influence of a modern State for the first time since 1919–21. How would he use this power to solve the national question, particularly what would be his approach to the North? What kind of social order would he aim at? What would be his policy towards the Church, and, above all, towards Britain in his aim for a United Republic?

As expected, his first actions, and they were swiftly enacted, were about constitutional aims. The Oath to the King was abolished, the Land Annuities retained, the status of the Governor-General who had appointed him was drastically reduced, and appeal to the Privy Council abolished. Another general election, a few months after victory, at a time when both his opponents and supporters expected his defeat brought him even further authority with an extra 130,000 votes and five extra seats, reducing Cosgrave's total to a mere 48. He won just under 50% of the total vote.

But then came a further development: the Economic War, with heavy duties on Irish exports to Britain, and retaliatory duties on British products into Ireland. He survived the resultant hardships, indeed using the opportunity to escalate protection and tillage extension, and measures to ease distress. Negotiations with Ramsay MacDonald and J. H. Thomas for Britain failed to ease the crisis, though a coal-cattle pact was an advance.

De Valera also dealt firmly and shrewdly with a "national front" of Cumann na nGael, the new centre party, and organisations with changing names, known generally as the Blue Shirts. The Blue Shirts organisation, led by Eoin O'Duffy, a former dismissed police commissioner, disintegrated within a year, but, in 1936, a challenge from sections of the I.R.A. had to be met. De Valera used similar measures against the I.R.A. which was becoming dissatisfied with his national policies.

That Economic War, however, stretched on for six years to 1938, causing economic and social problems which de Valera could not solve, emigration and unemployment reaching new levels though it could be said as promised that they were "relieved". De Valera, however, kept his lines to the British open, through quite an extraordinary series of meetings with Malcolm MacDonald, Secretary of the Commonwealth Relations Office, particularly when Neville Chamberlain replaced Stanley Baldwin as Prime Minister. It was this which enabled de Valera to effect one of the shrewdest moves of his life. He used the abdication of King Edward VIII on December 9, 1936 to do so.

By this means he removed, perhaps, the most fundamental Article of the Treaty, deleting that Article which bound Ireland's allegiance to the Crown. Kind Edward's application was officially sent to him as the Head of a British Dominion, but though he delayed his decision, he used the opportunity—on the advice of Seán MacEntee—to pass through the Dáil, the External Relations Act which removed the King from the Constitution except for "external" matters such as the appointment of ambassadors and such like. It can be noted that de Valera was the only Dominions Prime Minister who urged that Edward should remain King of England, but that Mrs. Simpson, the woman Edward loved, should not become queen. In that way was his famous Document No. 2 of 1922 implemented.

The first Fianna Fáil Cabinet, which took office in March, 1932. Seated (from left): Frank Aiken (Defence); P. J. Ruttledge (Lands and Fisheries); Eamon de Valera (President and External Affairs); Dr. J. Ryan (Agriculture); Tomás Derrig (Education); James Geoghegan (Justice). Standing (from left): Seán MacEntee (Finance); Seán T. O'Kelly (Vice-President, Local Government and Public Health); Senator J. Connolly (Posts and Telegraphs); Seán Lemass (Industry and Commerce); G. Boland, (Parliamentary Secretary to the President and to the Minister for Defence).

Ireland was now a sovereign State in "external association with Britain". Only the Treaty ports now remained as a threat to Irish neutrality in a world war. And two years later they too were recovered.

This was effected through the Anglo-Irish Agreement of 1938, the most significant national event even during those years of decision. That agreement between de Valera and Chamberlain, not alone secured the return of the ports, it also ended the Economic War, solved the Land Annuities issue, and concluded a satisfactory trade agreement. During those talks also, Chamberlain told de Valera that he believed that "Partition was an anomaly", but that admission was private, not official. Ireland had become a Republic and its neutrality, it seemed, could hardly be challenged effectively in the event of another world war.

In the short span of six years de Valera had abolished the Treaty, and the Civil War was over so far as the issues which dominated it were concerned. And all that had been accomplished without physical force. He had demonstrated that the political party was more powerful than the gun, that ballots were more effective than bullets. Partition was the "only outstanding issue" and a campaign was launched—on de Valera's initiative and with Chamberlain's approval—in Britain to bring the injustice of partition before the people. Unfortunately a new I.R.A., led by militants, chose that moment to launch a terrorist-bombing attack on people in British cities, an action which faced de Valera with a mini-civil war in Ireland for the duration of the Second World War which began the following year. But for that intervention something might have been won to improve the civil rights of the 500,000 Catholics in Northern Ireland, the only section of the Irish people who had gained nothing by all the agreements from 1921 onwards.

The Blue Shirts, a fascist-type movement recruited from former officers and men of the Free State Army, came to prominence in the early Thirties under General Eoin O'Duffy who had been relieved of his post as Commissioner of Police by de Valera. The movement fell asunder when the Fine Gael parliamentary party ended its association with O'Duffy.

Detente in 1938 . . . Anthony Eden (later Lord Avon and British Prime Minister) visiting de Valera at Government Buildings. From 1937 the two forged an abiding respect and understanding for the other; their friendship helped to ease some of the problems of Ireland's neutrality during the Second World War.

De Valera on his first flight on November 21, 1936. His pilot for the short trip over Dublin from Baldonnel was the American aviator, Colonel Charles Lindbergh, who made the first non-stop solo flight across the Atlantic in 1927.

The return of the Treaty
Ports in 1938: De Valera
accompanied by Cabinet
colleagues and senior officers
of the Army arriving at
Spike Island in Cork
harbour for the formal
handing-over of the British
base.

Jubilant British troops
leaving Spike Island.

As President of the Council of the League of Nations, de Valera presided over the Disarmament Conference at Geneva in September, 1932. At the table (from left): Baron von Neurath (Germany), M. Paul Boncour (France), President de Valera (Irish Free State), and Sir Eric Drummond and Sir John Simon (United Kingdom).

Installing of Dr. Douglas Hyde, founder of the Gaelic League, as the first President of Ireland in June, 1938. Seán T. O'Kelly (seated right) became Hyde's successor in 1945; de Valera followed O'Kelly into the office in 1959.

Dr. Douglas Hyde as the new President of Ireland entertaining Sinéad and Eamon de Valera at Áras an Uachtaráin, the former vice-regal lodge in Phoenix Park, Dublin.

The war-lords defied

Once asked by historians of which achievements he was most proud de Valera replied: "The Constitution of 1937 and the Anglo-Irish Agreement of 1938". He might have added the External Relations Act of 1936, for it must have been the most impudent piece of opportunism ever to have been perpetrated in such dangerous territory and at such a sensitive, even intimate, time for Britain—the abdication of its king because of his love for a woman. The Irish issue, of course, was nothing less than that which was the fundamental cause of the Civil War—the source of British authority in Ireland. In that case, certainly, de Valera's diplomacy was far superior—a million light-years away from the naked blunt gun which wasted so many lives and gained nothing.

The Constitution of 1937, in a national sense proclaiming the State's sovereignty and independence, with the External Relations Act and the return of the ports by the 1938 Agreement, all added up to a Republic of Ireland (Twenty-six Counties). The national aims had been achieved for that Irish State. But Partition remained, along with a deep and dangerous bitterness between the Protestant and the Catholic communities of Northern Ireland.

De Valera in 1938 was by no means in a strong position in Government. In the 1937 general election he had lost 100,000 votes and eight seats and was without an overall Dáil majority. The new Constitution had not been accepted by anything like an overwhelming majority. The figures were: 685,105 for the Constitution: 526,945 against: and about a third of those on the register did not vote. The people of Northern Ireland, of course, were not asked to vote. As the world moved closer to war de Valera must have viewed that uncertain situation with anxiety.

So when that new Anglo-Irish treaty was debated in the Dáil and approved, the politician took over from the statesman and, though the new President, Dr. Douglas Hyde, is said to have at first demurred at calling a new election, he did do so, and de Valera secured a massive 51% of the total poll. That election gave him an overall

De Valera at the time of the enactment of the new Constitution in 1937.

Dáil majority of 16. Whatever national mistakes he had made—in the Treaty, in the Civil War, or concerning the Oath—the 1938 election confirmed the confidence of the vote of 1933 in de Valera's leadership. He was their man for the national crisis arising out of war which broke upon the world in September 1939.

Resisted every threat

Whatever critics may say of de Valera—about the North, about his social, economic cultural, religious policies or his ambivalence about the I.R.A. or attitudes towards women or the language—there will be few to dispute his superb handling of Ireland's neutrality during the Second World War. Assailed by threats of conscription to the North on at least two occasions, of invasion by both Britain and the United States, of disruption or war by Hitler, he managed through sheer diplomacy and courage to save most of Ireland from horrors which afflicted the rest of the world. A reading of the

Inspecting the 1941 Army parade in Dublin marking the 25th anniversary of the 1916 Rising.

history of the relations between Ireland and the big Powers involved at that time, cannot but evoke deep admiration. His speech defending Ireland's neutrality on November 16, 1943, when under pressure from both the Allies and Hitler, was superb for its analysis, calm and courage.

Hitler's threat in 1943 had been in reply to de Valera's despatch of Dublin fire brigade units to a Belfast bombed by the Luftwaffe. That decision, so terribly important for a neutral country, was taken utterly on his own responsibility.

There is no doubt that he wished for the defeat of Nazism. Tens of thousands of Irish fought on the Allies' side or worked in British factories or services. British and Irish Army officers did work out forms of defence in case of a German invasion. A blind eye was turned to crashed British pilots finding their way over the Border or to British aircraft flying over Irish territory. Behind the scenes, too, there were

tough sessions with the British about supplies and arms, and particularly on those threats of occupation.

When at the end of the war, Churchill, in his famous victory speech, sneered at Ireland's neutrality, de Valera's reply was something of which even his enemies were proud. Churchill's words were unworthy of the man and not in accordance with the facts. De Valera responded calmly, even paying him compliments. He expressed his admiration for Britain "standing alone", but, *"There is a small nation that has stood alone not for one year or two, but for several hundred years, against aggression, a small nation that could never be forced to accept defeat, and that has never surrendered her soul. . . . It is hard for the strong to be just to the weak . . . By resisting the temptation to invade Ireland, Churchill, instead of adding another chapter to the bloodstained record of relations between England and this country, has advanced the cause of international morality."*

The record shows that de Valera stood up to the powerful United States and to Germany. He made an international protest to Hitler against the Nazis' invasion of Holland and Belgium; he protested vigorously against the bombing of Dublin by German aircraft; he insisted on the German embassy surrendering its radio transmitter when he considered it threatened Irish neutrality; he resisted offers of arms from Germany when Britain had restricted supplies; he acted shrewdly when Churchill seemed to be offering a proposal for a United Ireland in exchange for the ending of neutrality and refused to be drawn.

The one criticism which had wide backing concerned de Valera's handling of the new generation of the I.R.A. led by a member of the older "terrorist" wing, Seán Russell. In close touch with the Germans, the I.R.A. saw Germany as winning the war and then ending partition and was prepared to collaborate to some extent in sabotage in Britain and in Northern Ireland, though, in fact, little action of that kind took place. I.R.A. activities in Britain in early 1939–1940, however, when it bombed cities like London, Manchester, Birmingham and Coventry, killing many citizens, forced de Valera to take action. For almost five years of the war a miniature civil war went on in Ireland. In the Curragh Internment Camp I.R.A. men sang for joy as Hitler swept through Western Europe.

Hundreds of I.R.A. suspects were interned or imprisoned under emergency laws. Sixteen men were tried on murder charges by the Special Criminal Court, or the military court which had the power to inflict one sentence—death. Six men were shot or hanged, four received life imprisonment when their death sentences were commuted while others were jailed. Three I.R.A. men died on hunger-strike when de Valera refused to release them, another 12 were shot in armed combat in which about a dozen detectives died.

All the efforts of German agents were foiled, largely by good detective work. Only one agent, Goertz, eluded arrest for any considerable period, and he was ultimately captured.

On Hitler's death in his Berlin bunker, de Valera paid a formal call of condolence to Dr. Edouard Hempel, the German Minister in Dublin. His action led to a storm of protest.

Dr. Edouard Hempel, the German Minister to Ireland during the Second World War. De Valera tendered formally his condolences to the envoy on the death of Adolf Hitler.

De Valera said later: "Not to have done so would have been an act of unpardonable discourtesy to the German people and to Dr. Hempel." Most would consider that 'balancing act' to be too adroit by half, and one finds the act impossible to justify considering the scope of Hitler's crimes.

Celebrations at the G.P.O. during Easter Week 1949 to mark the coming into operation of the Republic of Ireland Act. The decision to sever the State's association with the British Commonwealth was undertaken by the Coalition Government shortly after it came to power in 1948. Controversy surrounded the move from its beginnings (the decision was leaked to the Sunday Independent and confirmed by the Taoiseach, John A. Costello, who was then visiting Canada). In the Dáil de Valera voiced his opposition to the constitutional change, principally on the grounds that it would make reunification of the country more difficult; however Fianna Fáil supported the Government's Bill for repeal of the External Relations Act of 1936. De Valera and his colleagues declined to participate in the celebrations which greeted the coming into force of the Republic of Ireland Act.
The British Government reacted sharply: Clement Attlee, the Prime Minister, assured the Northern Ireland Government that while citizens of the Twenty-Six Counties would not be regarded as foreigners by Britain, there would be no question of ending Partition without the consent of the Stormont Parliament. Westminster enshrined this guarantee in the Ireland Act 1949.

The advent of Coalition Government

As the war ended the Labour movement posed a challenge to de Valera on the Trade Union Act of 1941, which sought to rationalise trade union opposition to the Wages Standstill Orders. The orders had allowed prices to exceed wage increases by 33%. A rejuvenated Labour Party, and a new farmers' party, Clann na Talmhan, challenged de Valera in the 1943 general election: Fianna Fáil lost ten seats and more than 100,000 votes. With a split in the Labour Party, however, and after renewed threats by Britain and the United States, the Government won back a year later nine of the ten seats and almost 50% of the total vote. Labour, split into 'National' and official wings, lost five seats.

De Valera raised the question of Partition once more with Britain. He threatened to repeal the External Relations' Act if something was not done to seek to restore the Council of Ireland, the proposal which had been abolished in 1925, his aim being to win full civil rights for Northern Catholics or to secure a form of an Ireland united.

There were signs too that nations were turning towards radical social reform and seeking new leaders. Churchill, the man who had won the war, was defeated overwhelmingly in the British general election even as the Beveridge Plan for the brave new world was being announced.

In Ireland, similar social plans began to appear. De Valera, now in 1947–48, had been in power for 16 continuous years and seemed unable to cope with the rising social discontent. Even the national teachers went on strike in 1946 for several months. They were followed by bank clerks, journalists and many other workers seeking wage increases to offset living costs.

The most significant political development of the 1946–48 period was the rise of a new Republican Party, Clann na Poblachta, with a leader, Seán MacBride, whose charisma, to some extent, resembled that of de Valera. He was a former I.R.A. Chief-of-Staff, son of the famous Maud Gonne and of John MacBride who was executed in Easter Week. His party, like

Seán MacBride, a prominent member of the Irish Bar, led the emergence of a new republican party, Clann na Poblachta, in 1946. He was given the External Affairs portfolio in the first Inter-Party Government, 1948–51.

many republican parties, gave the impression of being socially radical and it harmonised with programmes from the Labour Party, Fine Gael and Clann na Talmhan whose basis was the small farmer of the west. Prices and social reform were the main issues of the 1948 election. De Valera's days of national crisis and glory were over, it seemed. The rise of MacBride's party was the great threat to de Valera essentially because of its appeal to Republican voters. In what his colleagues claim was the one single electoral misjudgement of his political life, he suddenly announced a general election, seeking to wrong-foot Clann na Poblachta before it was fully ready. That election gave de Valera 68 seats, eight seats less than in 1944. The Opposition parties, securing a total of 769,000 votes, secured 75 seats.

Though he had the largest party, and Fianna Fáil was, therefore, expected to form the new

Government, he was outwitted when the opposition parties and Independents combined to defeat him in the election of Taoiseach, and John A. Costello became head of the first Inter-Party Government.

In defeat de Valera turned to the issue of Partition. He had no intention of competing with the programmes of the Coalition parties for social reform. To his mind the ending of Partition would open the only way to social reform—in a United Ireland. And so he, and his closest comrade, Frank Aiken, began a world tour to explain the injustice of Partition to the world, in Australia, and the other Dominions and in Britain itself. Somehow that had to become the issue again in Ireland and so it was that all speeches made abroad were reported at home in Ireland. In a sense his strategy succeeded for that propaganda could have been a factor in persuading the new Government to repeal the External Relations' Act, thus breaking the very last, slender link between Ireland and the Commonwealth. Ireland became a Republic through a Government which had as its

dominant sector, the old Commonwealth Fine Gael. The Government was trying to be more Republican than de Valera. The "Ireland Bill" in Britain, strengthening the Unionist position, did make Partition an issue, uniting all parties in a new campaign, which inevitably was followed by a new I.R.A.

Mother-and-child controversy

The new Government did introduce some social reforms, particularly in health and housing, but it was soon in difficulty with the Catholic bishops on health legislation. Paradoxically, when the legislation had been passed through the Dáil de Valera ignored a protest by the Hierarchy against the section introducing a new mother-and-child service, free of charge. The new Government, for all its alleged radicalism, took it far more seriously, and the Minister for Health, Dr. Noel Browne, was forced by MacBride to resign when he refused to abandon his scheme. De Valera, seeing in this a possible road back to power, allowed his party interests to reign above national interests and remained

Seán MacBride, his son and his mother, the legendary and indefatigable Maud Gonne. Her husband, Major John MacBride, was executed along with the leaders of the 1916 Rising.

Cabinet members of the first Inter-Party Government, 1948: Seated (from left)—Seán MacBride (Clann na Poblachta), John A. Costello (Fine Gael), General Richard Mulcahy (F.G.), Dr. T. O'Higgins (F.G.). Standing— William Norton (Labour), Joseph Blowick (Clann na Talmhan), General Seán Mac Eoin (F.G.), James Dillon (Independent).

silent through one of the most controversial Dáil debates on Church–State politics in Ireland. The debate vastly interested the Northern Protestants who saw in practice what they had believed—Home Rule means Rome Rule. A contribution from de Valera at such a time could have been of enormous national value, but all he said in the Dáil when asked to speak was: *"I think we have heard enough"*. Only the Government parties, now riven by the issue, had participated in the debate.

The debate, coming as it did after the fiercest anti-Partition campaign ever, made a farce of that campaign, as a Government and a Parliament bowed the knee to the Crozier. As Seán Ó Faoláin said: *"We can now roll up the map of Ireland. We shall not be needing it again."*

De Valera was to regain power by eroding the appeal of the Inter-Party Government and winning the support of the Independents. He was returned in the 1951 election and continued to rule for three years on such a basis. But again he was to introduce a hair-shirt budget, and in the 1954 election received his lowest number of seats since 1932. It looked as if his twilight hour had arrived. It was the time also when his eyesight began to get worse. It had been failing since 1951, and after hopes had been high following an operation in Utrecht, it failed almost completely. It left him with less than peripheral vision.

Yet, in the 1957 general election, forced by an economic crisis, de Valera, then aged 75 and in spite of almost total blindness, campaigned vigorously and incredibly achieved his greatest victory—securing 78 seats with almost 600,000 votes. Fianna Fáil now had an overall majority of nine seats, winning 10 from Fine Gael, seven

Dr. Noel Browne, Minister for Health in the first Inter-Party Government, was forced to resign by MacBride when he refused to abandon his controversial free-for-all Mother-and-Child scheme.

from Labour, two from Clann na Talmhan. Except for one nominal seat, the entire Clann na Poblachta party was wiped out, including its leader, MacBride. The only other party which gained in that election was Sinn Féin, the fruit of the Republic Act of 1949. Sinn Féin's abstention from the Dáil gave de Valera an overall majority of 13.

Time to stand down

But as 1958 ended, his closest colleagues, like Seán Lemass, were to tell political correspondents that *"Dev's old magic is going. He has become the adjudicator among Ministers, no longer the initiator."* Oscar Traynor, Seán MacEntee and Jim Ryan approached him to discuss a candidate for the coming presidential election. Traynor said: "If you are not the candidate then we will lose the Presidency". De Valera, aware that his colleagues were telling him, kindly, that they thought it best he should go, replied *"I am at the disposal of the party".*

Shortly afterwards he announced to a private meeting of Fianna Fáil that he had decided to stand as its presidential candidate and that he would retire as Taoiseach and as party president. It was an emotional scene and tears were in evidence, both in the presidential chair and in the hall. He also shocked the parliamentary members that day when he said he intended putting through a Bill to abolish Proportional Representation voting in favour of the direct vote. There would be one deputy in each constituency; not the three to seven, or more, seats as under P.R.

The Bill to amend the voting system led to a major debate in the Dáil and Senate. De Valera opened with a tour-de-force speech: the P.R. system, he claimed, created too many small political parties, as in many European countries, and brought democracy into disrepute and caused unstable government. Both Fine Gael and Labour contested the Bill over several weeks. To many speakers the proposal seemed to abandon the aim of a united Ireland, P.R. always having been held out as some form of guarantee of fair treatment of minorities. Finally, it was accepted by the Dáil but rejected by the Senate, and returned to the Dáil for further debate.

De Valera closed the final debate on May 26, 1959. It was his last Dáil speech in his last political battle in more than 40 years. His performance in the Dáil that evening, and his last few moments in the Dáil Chamber, remain among the most vivid memories of my years as a political correspondent.

The speech of 'The Grand Old Man' of Irish politics, now in his 77th year and almost blind, demonstrated that he could still be supreme. He spoke without notes for more than an hour, quoting Burke's famous Bristol speech, defining the role of the M.P. Were members to be leaders, loyal to their own informed and critical judgement or mere ambassadors, messengers of their constituents? De Valera was with Burke, urging deputies to think with their minds, not with their votes, to use their own judgement in the national interest.

His finest moment came when he purported to read from a Fine Gael journal in which an article denounced Coalition government, necessarily consisting of many parties, and that a plurality

De Valera speaking at a College Green rally during the 1959 Presidential election. He was elected with a majority of more than 120,000 votes, but the people rejected his proposal to abolish Proportional Representation voting.

of parties was the direct result of P.R. Holding the journal before him, and purporting to read from it—but actually quoting from memory—the blind Taoiseach unwittingly held the journal page the wrong way up. Everyone else in the House was aware of it and the 'deception' added rather than diminished the drama of the occasion. Later still in the debate, as if he sensed what had happened, taking up another journal, he said *"how dearly I wish I could read all of this article to you."* But he explained the arguments it used against P.R. and coalition. It had been written by a former Cumann na nGael Minister, Ernest Blythe. Here de Valera was seeking to win Fine Gael voters to his proposal.

Later, after the debate had ended with victory for the Government, came his last visit to the Chamber. As the Dáil was adjourned for the Referendum campaign and Presidential election, its business ended and the Chamber emptied, I noticed from the Press Gallery that he had remained behind in his seat as Leader of the Government. Then as the lights dimmed, he stood up and walked up the stairs slowly, steadying himself on the hand-rail. At the door, he paused and looked around at what could have been to him only a blurred outline of the Chamber in which he had been such a dominant figure for almost 33 years.

He was to be elected President by 538,000 votes to 417,536 for General Seán MacEoin the Fine Gael candidate. The people, however, rejected his proposal to abolish P.R. by a big majority. The cause of that rejection was attributed to the reluctance of his own deputies to work for a victory. The price he asked—their Dáil seat—was too high. The result was described as a "PRhic" victory.

Intransigent on the Northern Question

On all issues and problems of strictly national-sovereign status, and on the wider fields of international crises, there can be little doubt that de Valera was the greatest Irishman of his era.

Historians do not stop at the frontiers of a country or at the story of a nation's fight for freedom. They study also the policies applied to secure the happiness, prosperity and security of the whole people. Historians will criticise de Valera for the society which his regimes created in the internal life of the independent, sovereign Irish State. Their criticism will be all the more severe because of the role which that society was bound to play towards the solution, or the worsening, of the problem of the Partition. De Valera said in 1933 that his solution for that problem was to try to make the conditions in the Republic so attractive that the North would wish to come in. But it did not turn out quite like that.

The areas of most importance in Ireland during de Valera's era were social, economic, cultural, ethical, matters of private conscience, Church-State relations, attitudes to the I.R.A. (or the descendants of the many fragments styling themselves I.R.A. since the Civil War) the Language; and political matters which had a direct bearing on Northern Ireland.

On the social and economic problems, which were acute enough in the new State when de Valera took over in 1932, there had been hopes that he would provide radical social re-construction. He had declared that if solutions of social problems were impossible within the existing system he would go outside it. In his famous League of Nations' speech in 1932 he promised the overhaul of the systems of production, distribution, finance and exchange and said that not to do so would be to fail "ignobly and disastrously". Much progress was made within the limits of private enterprise, including giant State enterprises, ambitious housing programmes were completed, social welfare and health and education services improved and vast schemes for agriculture organised. But the problems of acute poverty, unemployment and heavy emigration were never resolved completely.

One imagined de Valera, as the son of a poor Irish emigrant mother, being inspired by a passion to end all emigration, yet during his long regime, many thousands had to emigrate in search of work. His early promise of over-hauling the economy was not fully realised, and unemployment, emigration, inadequate housing and social services were permanent problems in his day.

Role of Catholic Church

It was far from being the State to which Northerners, Protestant or Catholic, were attracted: the ethical and cultural framework of the Free State did not help forward any reconciliation with the North nor any material or cultural enrichment of the people of the South. Many had hoped that de Valera, with his anti-clerical battles over national questions, would halt the Catholic character of the State built by Cosgrave from 1922 to 1932, but the new Constitution of 1937 proved to be disappointing. It strengthened rather than weakened Church influence, giving the Catholic Church a "special position" above other Churches, and applied Catholic social principles in relation to censorship, education, public ownership and other social issues. It gave nourishment to the worst loyalist elements in the North in their assertion that "Home Rule was Rome Rule". In addition the Constitution also contained a provocative claim to Northern Ireland.

Northerners were always quick to see that Catholic social principles also governed laws and attitudes in the areas of co-education, non-denominational schools, management of schools, child adoption, dancing hours, drinking hours, juvenile delinquency, industrial schools, hospital ethics, contraception and in many other areas of daily living.

The Constitution banned divorce completely and strengthened censorship of books and films. It also had a paternalistic attitude towards women—though some provisions turned out to be liberally interpreted. On the economic side,

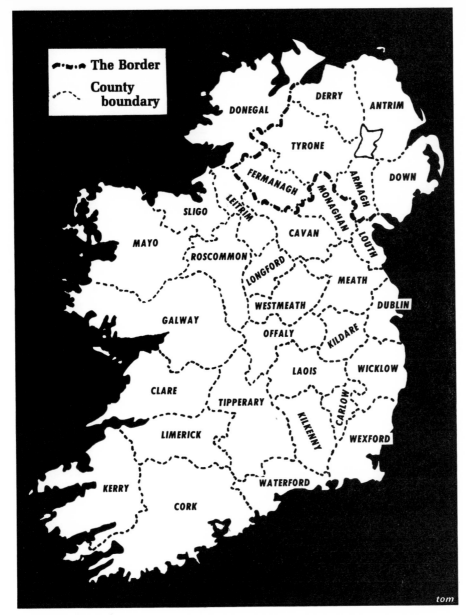

The partitioning of Ireland—six north-eastern counties under the jurisdiction of the Belfast Parliament—was instigated by Lloyd George in 1916 and was established de facto after the failure of the Boundary Commission in 1922.

the Constitution safeguarded private property, making public ownership much more difficult than under the Free State Constitution. Another blow at Northern accord was that the English language was given second place to Irish. A consistent view at the time was that the Constitution consolidated Partition though de Valera believed it held out important concessions towards the North. He saw it as the basis for a future united Ireland, he said. But he also did say that were he ever offered an Irish-speaking State of 26 Counties or a united Ireland without the language, he would accept the former. The first place in his heart was the language, not unity. He said often if he were offered the option of the language or freedom he would

After the unveiling of a plaque in D'Olier Street, Dublin, in April, 1967 to the memory of Seán Mac Diarmada, one of the 1916 signatories (Mac Diarmada had an office in the block from where he managed and edited the I.R.B. organ, Irish Freedom.) The group included Colonel Seán Brennan, aide-de-camp; Denis McCullough, Dr. James Ryan, Mr. and Mrs. Eamonn de hOir, Joseph O'Doherty, Harry Nicholls, Professor Liam Ó Briain, Mr. and Mrs. Richard Mulcahy, Mrs. Seán T. O'Kelly, Frank Daly, Alec McCabe, Cathal O'Shannon, Mrs. Ruttledge, Mrs. Carrie Daly, Tom O'Reilly and Seán Thompson.

prefer the language: freedom could be obtained later, but a dead language could never be recovered.

In the South, however, the principles governing living standards and the freedom of the individual conscience proved inferior to those prevailing in the North on issues not connected with the Border. It did not help that Northern Protestants saw their neighbours aiming at a Catholic, socially-conservative, Gaelic-speaking, anti-English state, something utterly alien to ideals of even the most liberal and moderate Protestants. Publicly de Valera demonstrated that he blamed Britain for Partition, for creating it and maintaining it by force and subsidies. He apparently did not see any role for the North's million Protestants, merely pawns to be handed over, and having no right in determining their own future. He once urged they should be "bought over" to the country of their choice. As the issue would not be determined in the North, the 500,000 Nationalists there were offered no strategy except to work for unity, a policy which isolated them from the many radical progressive socialists, Labour and Liberal Protestants who tried to unite against hardcore loyalism to secure social and civil reforms. Such Protestants received little encouragement from Northern Nationalists or Republicans. Protestant allies were not needed. Britain would decide. It is now only too clear that a whole nation, or, at least, a whole generation was utterly wrong.

Political paradox

There were others who sensed the political paradox. Some of de Valera's own Ministers fought in Cabinet for a more plural society on the lines of that envisaged by Wolfe Tone in which the guiding principle was reconciliation of Protestant and Catholic. In the Dáil Frank MacDermot urged that no progress was possible *"while we regard Northern Protestants as not worth persuading, not worth convincing, not worth understanding"*. He accused de Valera of exploiting the North's Catholic minority, and its great desire for a united Ireland, simply to maintain his party in power by proclaiming unity as his aim, but without any will or strategy to achieve it.

And so it was that this man of undoubted genius in national, international, and other fields, failed to make progress towards implementing the first aim of his life and of his Fianna Fáil party. His whole life's achievement was diminished by that failure, almost certainly caused by his conservative social, economic, cultural and political policies inside Ireland. Can that failure be explained by the probability that indeed he had applied his mind to the North, but concluded that unity, or reconciliation in the North, were both impossible? If that were his conclusion then one could understand completely that his only alternative was to build the 26-county State. Not being a Socialist, he built it on private enterprise lines, though with conservative restraint, since the Irish independence movement was not Socialist. It was not the first colonial revolt but the last bourgeois-nationalist, bourgeois-Catholic uprising in Western Europe with its *raison d'etre* to build private enterprise in Ireland.

The nation must be grateful to him for defining its aspirations, but critics may say the real tragedy of modern Ireland is that this great man did not use all his stature, authority and brilliance, to change even slightly a nation's Catholic conservative thinking on the North.

De Valera was great because his words "echoed the songs in the hearts of the people". The songs of his generation were songs of sacrifice, victory or even death for Ireland, songs of national freedom for Catholic Ireland. The songs of new generations may be of a new patriotism, of reconciliation between Irishmen of all religions, or none; songs of freedom of private conscience, and diversity of culture, songs, above all, of a new humanity.

The tragedy of Ireland may have been that de Valera while the greatest leader in the struggle for national independence was also a dedicated conservative deeply committed to outmoded Catholic social principles. The glory of Ireland, however, was the Independence Movement which he led from 1917 to July 1921. It is for other men to complete the freedom which he won.

De Valera at 89 taking the salute during the 55th anniversary of the Rising. In the North sectarian violence continued to mount.

Eamon de Valera became the third President of Ireland in June, 1959 and served two terms of seven years in office. On his retirement in 1973 he and his wife took to the seclusion of the Linden convalescent home at Talbot Lodge, Blackrock, Co. Dublin, for their remaining years.

The Presidential years

In his 82nd year, de Valera, as President of the Republic of Ireland, made a triumphant return in May, 1964 to the United States, the land of his birth, and addressed a joint session of Congress. President Lyndon Johnson said: "You belong to us just as Kennedy in a very special way belonged to Ireland. It is a great honour to welcome you home."

It was a poignant moment for de Valera, who less than a year before had welcomed President Kennedy to his country, and who a few months later attended the assassinated President's funeral in Arlington National Cemetery.

But drama and poignancy marked de Valera's long career, and his accession to the Presidency in 1959 did not alter the pattern. He received many eminent statesmen and, indeed, thousands of ordinary visitors found little difficulty in meeting him at Aras an Uachtaráin. He travelled much within the country, and found it difficult to refuse invitations to official and unofficial functions.

He attended or was represented at funerals of old comrades in the freedom fight, and visited many of them in hospitals and nursing homes.

During his Presidency he received many distinctions at home and abroad. In 1960 de Valera, Chancellor of the National University of Ireland, received an honorary doctorate from the University of Dublin. At the conferring, Professor W. B. Stanford said: "You have placed the coping stone on the walls of our political independence."

His 80th birthday in 1962 was noted around the world, and among the first congratulatory messages was one from Queen Elizabeth of Britain. The *Sunday Times* said he was a man who demanded to belong, who demanded nationality and where there was no country to contain that nationality, he made one. And the *Guardian* remarked: "He has so acted as to bring us, too, on this side of the Irish Sea to think of him not as an enemy deserving respect, but as a friend."

Several million British television viewers

Bon voyage . . . joking with the 50 Aer Lingus air hostesses whom he received at Aras an Uachtaráin before their departure for the United States to take part in St. Patrick's Day parades in 1968.

Laying the foundation stone of the new Abbey in 1963. He once appeared on the Abbey stage — in "A Christmas Hamper" in 1905.

precedented step of warmly thanking the R.U.C. officers for their courtesy and assistance.

This was the year, too, when arrangements were made for the completion of the President's authorised biography. Mr. Thomas O'Neill, of University College, Galway, was appointed to succeed Frank Gallagher, whose death interrupted the research necessary for this undertaking.

In June, 1963, the President of the United States, 47-year-old John Fitzgerald Kennedy— the grandson of Irish emigrants—arrived for a four-day state visit. For both Presidents it was a signal occasion. For the people of Ireland, as the Kennedy cavalcade wound its way to Wexford, Cork, Limerick and Galway, it was an hour of glory and national pride. As he departed, Kennedy said: "I did not know 'fáilte' could mean so much."

In January, 1964, he was made an honorary fellow of the Royal College of Surgeons of Ireland.

In May he set off on his first official visit as President of Ireland to the U.S.A. to be acclaimed in the cities he visited, with a ticker-tape welcome in Washington. He was the guest of President Lyndon Johnson at Blair House, and his public appearances included the 20-minute address to Congress.

A hope of the future

The central theme of his address dealt with the continued division of Ireland. Before he sat down to a tremendous ovation, President de Valera expressed the hope that some day another President of Ireland might be able to stand in the American Parliament and say "our severed country has been united, and the last source of enmity between British people and the Irish people has been removed, and at last we can be truly friends."

After the American visit, which included two journeys to Boston and attendance at the World Fair, where he visited the Irish pavilion, the President journeyed to Canada for a three-day State visit. During these trips his amazing stamina did not fail him, though those close to him noticed he was tired. It was known that his medical advisers had not been in favour of such an extensive tour, but this did not affect his desire to revisit the country of his birth.

He was a man who met many of the greats of

watched him speak to Fyffe Robertson in a B.B.C. telecast on his 80th birthday. As could be expected he chose to comment on a subject which, like the revival of the Irish language, was near to his heart. Partition, he said, was ". . . a heartbreak, more especially since a large majority in that area do not want it."

In March, 1962, on St. Patrick's Day (which marked the end of the Patrician Year) de Valera, during a 10-day State visit to Italy, received from Pope John XXIII the Supreme Order of Christ—the highest order of Papal distinction.

In 1963, the President was given a special R.U.C. escort when he travelled to Armagh to attend the funeral of his old friend, John Cardinal D'Alton. That journey took place through a snow blizzard, and de Valera took the un-

On his retirement from the Presidency in June, 1973, de Valera paid a last visit to the Dáil, scene of so many of his parliamentary battles over a span of 33 years.

his day: Churchill, Nehru, de Gaulle, four Popes, leaders of nations in the East and West, and the men who made and broke the League of Nations. Memorable visitors to Dublin during his Presidency included: Prince Rainier and Princess Grace of Monaco; the President of Pakistan, Field-Marshal Ayub Khan; the Prime Minister of Mauritius, Dr. Ramgoolan; the French Minister of Foreign Affairs, M. Couve de Murville, and Senator Edward Kennedy.

In August, 1964, while on a visit to the Co. Clare agricultural show, he opened a museum in Ennis, the centre of his many election victories.

In spite of his intensity, he was not without a sense of humour. When laying the foundation stone of the new Abbey Theatre, he revealed that the tall, thin, dark young man who appeared in "A Christmas Hamper" in 1905 and whom *The Irish Times* on that occasion described as "cadaverous", was none other than himself.

The visit to the White House (left) on November 26, 1963, to meet the new U.S. President, Lyndon Johnson, the day following the funeral of John F. Kennedy who was assassinated in Dallas.

Visiting Pope John XXIII on St. Patrick's Day, 1962. In all he was received in private audience by four pontiffs, three of whose coronations he attended.

Princess Caroline, daughter of Prince Rainier and Princess Grace of Monaco, during a visit to Aras an Uachtaráin in August, 1963.

De Valera and Jack Lynch, the Fianna Fáil leader who was a formidable hurling player in his day, showing King Baudouin the art of hurling during the Belgian monarch's State visit with Queen Fabiola to Dublin in May, 1968.

Entertaining General Charles de Gaulle during the French leader's private visit for a holiday in Kerry in June, 1969.

Before his retirement from the Presidency in 1973, de Valera enjoyed the distinction of being the oldest serving head-of-state in the world. No statesman of the 20th century can be said to have centred his life so totally on his religion: a devout Catholic, he accepted unreservedly the teachings of the Church, but in matters political he set a sharp limit to the guidance he accepted from the Hierarchy.

Old friends meeting in the rain
. . . de Valera and his
Presidential successor, Erskine
Childers, at Arbour Hill in May
1974. Son of the distinguished
author and patriot, Childers died in
office in the following November.

De Valera, who steadfastly
refused to write an autobiography,
lent his assistance and papers to
the Earl of Longford and
Thomas P. O'Neill; their
authorised biography was
published in 1970.

Host of the Nation

Whatever may be said about de Valera and his political career, it must be noted that as President of Ireland he had all the qualities one could ask for. He lent a quiet dignity, courtesy and old-world charm to the office and was a father of the people.

The highlight of his 14 years in office was when he acted as host to John F. Kennedy, the American President, in June, 1963. They got on like old friends, while Bean Sinéad de Valera, then aged 85, captivated the young President. The President and his wife were greatly distressed a few months later when Kennedy was assassinated. De Valera, then 81, attended the funeral in Washington.

A year later de Valera again visited Washington, this time as the guest of the American nation. He addressed both Houses of the U.S. Congress and appealed to all to work for peace everywhere.

That visit was in sharp contrast to his journey in 1919 when he arrived in New York, a stowaway in the hold of a ship, and had to remain in hiding for several weeks. Then he had sought, in vain, for American recognition of the newly-formed Irish Republic.

In 1969 he was host briefly to the French President, Charles de Gaulle, who, on a private visit to Ireland, spent June 17th at Aras an Uachtaráin. De Gaulle was absent for the first time in 24 years from the Paris celebrations on the anniversary of his call for French resistance against the Nazi occupation in 1940.

Another U.S. President, Richard Nixon, visited Ireland in October, 1970.

In 1967 de Valera had been made an honorary fellow of the Royal College of Physicians of Ireland and, a year later, a fellow of the Royal Society, the oldest scientific society in existence. On Palm Sunday, 1971, in his 89th year, he went to Lourdes, the Marian shrine in France.

He had been re-elected President in 1966, after an exhausting year in which he had attended all the State ceremonies associated with the 50th anniversary of the Easter Rising. In that election he had been opposed by a strong, young opponent, T. F. O'Higgins (now the Chief Justice). De Valera won with a lower majority of 10,000 votes, though receiving more votes than in 1959.

On January 6th, 1970, at a New Year Day's reception for the diplomatic corps at Aras an Uachtaráin, he urged all nations to unite in a solemn covenant for peace and to submit all international disputes to arbitration and judicial determination.

Although no formal acknowledgement was ever made it is known that he played a key part

De Valera with the veteran newspaperman, Michael McInerney, at one of their last meetings during his Presidency. McInerney was political correspondent of The Irish Times for 21 years from 1952 and wrote the ten-part account of de Valera's life and work contained in the first half of this book.

One highlight of de Valera's role as host of the nation was the visit of the U.S. President, John F. Kennedy, in 1963. The young American leader, descendant of Irish emigrants, was assassinated in Dallas later that year.

in resolving the deep cleavage inside the Fianna Fáil Government in May 1970 on the question of aid to the North. He supported Mr. Lynch unequivocally in those events, when his advice was sought on at least one occasion.

To the end he maintained a daily interest in all that happened, in the North and elsewhere in the world. In one of my last interviews with him he spoke of the death toll of 1,000 in the North's violence, of the hopelessness of armed force there. He spoke of his concern for world peace, and, surprisingly, of the problems of housing and industrial relations. He regretted that his Government's earlier failure to appreciate obsolescence in housing had caused the housing problems of today. He believed, he said, that the absence of a strong Labour Party was because Fianna Fáil, under Seán Lemass, had been the Labour Party. "But", he concluded, "when I think back to that day in 1898 when I came to Dublin first I remember Kingsbridge station and this place here (the Aras) were deep

in the countryside, and the trams were driven by horses. Now in this area there are tens of thousands of houses, many factories, churches, there is television and motor-cars, aeroplanes and all the rest. In 1898 I was a lad of 15 years. Now I am nearly blind, an old man of more than 90 years of age, so that I know nothing only what is read to me, or what I hear on radio or television, or what I hear from friends, and I say to myself, how can I give any opinion on anything. I don't know the facts." He was really asking to be left alone, and as I left him he stood up to say good-bye and remained standing until I had left the room.

When he retired ultimately in June, 1973, the streets of Dublin were lined with people as his car drove him from Phoenix Park to Blackrock and Linden. At Boland's Mills, scene of his 1916 effort, 30,000 gathered to hear his last public words. He continued to be active in attending functions and requiems for his old comrades until his death on August 29, 1975.

The Freedom of the City of Dublin was conferred jointly on de Valera and John A. Costello in March, 1975.
Mr. Costello, a distinguished constitutional lawyer and political opponent, told his listeners: "Both in and out of
office I received nothing but the utmost courtesy from Mr. de Valera."

In the final public address of his long career, de Valera spoke to the thousands who gathered at Boland's Mills on June 24, 1973, the day he left Aras an Uachtaráin to retire to Talbot Lodge.

A poignant moment as de Valera sympathised with the widow of Dermot Barry who died in 1972. Barry, a staff photographer with The Irish Times for 46 years, was a close friend of de Valera, and was the author of many of the photographs reproduced in this book.

91

De Valera was honoured in 1966 by the University of Louvain with a doctorate honoris causa in recognition of his work for the emancipation of the Irish people.

After his election to the Chancellorship of the National University of Ireland in December, 1921.

Symbol of the era he bestrode

by F. S. L. Lyons

Eamon De Valera has always been a problem to historians and will no doubt continue to be so for many years to come. More worshipped by his followers and more hated by his opponents than perhaps any figure in our history since Parnell (even Michael Collins, though of comparable stature, hardly evoked the same extremes of feeling), de Valera's longevity sets him apart from virtually everybody else. In the obvious sense that his direct involvement with politics ceased nearly 17 years ago, he belongs to the past. But since we had taken for granted his presence "in the Park" until relatively recently, we still cannot help thinking of him as a contemporary, which indeed, with his dignified and punctilious discharge of his Presidential functions, he was, up to the day of his departure.

The very fact that he lived so long in the public eye makes for a further difficulty of dealing with a man who not only means different things to different individuals and to different parties, but also means different things to different generations. It is not easy to discern where the watershed occurs. Some would put it at his assumption of office in 1932, others as late as 1939: I myself would guess that it falls about midway between those two dates. But in his case the distinction between the years of struggle and the years of power is much more than the ordinary distinction between rise and fulfilment that one might make for any successful politician. If the present generation has a view of de Valera which is not the view of his own generation (or of the survivors from that bygone age) this is because an age of revolution is fundamentally different from an age of consolidation. When a man succeeds in surviving from the years of violence to the years of peace we need not be surprised if, in the end, he comes to look like two—or in de Valera's case, three—different persons.

The first person of this fascinating trinity is the least complicated. If de Valera had been executed in 1916 he would have found a place in the revolutionary pantheon, but he would scarcely have been one of its most arresting exhibits. He would be remembered now with respect, but not, one suspects, with great vividness, as a scholar in his chosen field of mathematics, as a dedicated enthusiast for the Irish language, as a conscientious commander in the field, and, most of all, as a man who stood quietly but firmly on the rock of the Republic proclaimed on Easter Monday.

The idealist

Thereafter, events, combined with his own capacity for leadership, soon thrust him to the centre of the stage and under the arc lights that beat down upon him between 1917 and 1922 the second de Valera was gradually and painfully formed. This de Valera, of whom more than a trace remained to the end of his career, was an idealist—if you like, a doctrinaire—who was gradually driven by circumstance to come to terms with political reality, but in whom the prophet and the visionary were never entirely submerged. But although, as he once told me, a hopeless amateur when he won the East Clare election, he soon became the complete professional and almost at once began to display some of his most characteristic traits. One thinks immediately of the subtlety of the 1917 formula defining the aims of a greatly transformed Sinn Féin, of the dialectical skill he showed when he fenced so brilliantly with Lloyd George in the summer of 1921, and of his passionate and rigid adherence to principle, as he saw it, both during the Treaty negotiations and during the tragic debates which followed them.

Because those debates issued in the Civil War and because de Valera's part in the final breach was so crucial, it was of course this phase of his career which, more than anything else, brought down upon him the bitterness of the pro-Treaty party, a bitterness which was to permeate Irish politics for years to come and is still not wholly dead. Nowadays, we all recognise only too clearly what a deep wound the Civil War inflicted on our country but perhaps the time has come to suggest that for de Valera himself, as well as for the victims it claimed on either side, the conflict was an unmitigated catastrophe.

Concept too novel

It was a catastrophe in a double sense. First of all, in the debates which preceded the split, he failed to carry his concept of external association as embodied in Document No. 2—that is, the idea that an Irish Republic might be associated with the British Commonwealth for external purposes while remaining entirely independent in its own internal affairs. This idea was to have a distinguished future, but in 1922 it was still too novel to have the impact its author hoped. It was also, as some thought then, and many have felt since, too close to what the Treaty already conceded to justify the rigidity of his stance. Ironically, however, because it seemed to others to deviate too far from the "isolated" republic, the consequence of its rejection was that de Valera, if he was not to alienate his own supporters, found himself to an increasing extent encased in the strait-jacket of a republic which was not precisely his republic.

The second way in which the Civil War affected his own position was even more devastating. For what the struggle and its aftermath did to him was to introduce him brutally to the realities of power in a military situation, when civilian politicians count for very little. The nadir of his career was reached, as Lord Longford and T. P. O'Neill demonstrate in their biography, between the outbreak of the war in June 1922 and de Valera's arrest just over a year later. During that time, though the ostensible head of a Republican Emergency Government, his power to influence events was minimal and it is probable that the traumatic experience of that year had a permanent effect in shaping his later views about the proper

Tribute to Theobald Wolfe Tone . . . laying a wreath at the Bodenstown grave of the 1798 patriot.

republican position—which, as I have already been trying to suggest, he had effectively abandoned from the moment he had begun to define external association—and also from the doctrine, then staunchly held by diehards, that as the Second Dáil had never, in their view, ceased to exist, continuity of authority rested with Sinn Féin, diminished and fragmented though it was. The logical sequels to this increasing alienation were the breach with his old political colleagues (the I.R.A. had already gone its own way), the creation of Fianna Fáil and the fateful decision to enter the Dáil in 1927. Further down that same road he was to arrive, nine years later, at the point where he would act towards the I.R.A. in a manner not easily distinguishable from the way in which the Cosgrave Government had acted against that organisation in the previous decade.

Attention has centred, perhaps excessively, on the elaborate manoeuvres to which de Valera resorted in pursuit of his determination to resume parliamentary politics without seeming to have taken the parliamentary oath, but though these certainly throw a revealing light upon his mental processes, they are surely far less important than the all-important fact that by re-entering the mainstream of constitutional politics he had opened the way for an alternative government, thus contributing directly to the strengthening of democracy in this State.

External association
When he formed that alternative government in 1932 few would have dared to predict either that it would last for 16 years or that the man at its head would achieve an international reputation as one of the great conservatives of his time and thus complete the third and last of his transformations. In retrospect, the apprehensions aroused by his coming to power seem almost ludicrous, understandable though they were at the time. For although at first sight his initial clashes with the British government over the land annuities and the Oath of Allegiance seemed only too literal a fulfilment of those apprehensions, we can see how that both the economic war (harsh and probably unnecessary as were the sufferings it imposed on the nation) and the political quarrel were rooted in ideas which he, and others, had held for many years. The economic war, after all, accelerated rather

relationship which should exist between army and government.

The changed republican
The man who at the end of these tribulations was imprisoned by the Free Staters in 1923 must have seemed as nearly at the end of his tether as the man who had been imprisoned by the British in 1916. But in fact the second de Valera was very different from the first. He was vastly more experienced, perhaps more disillusioned, certainly more aware of the difficulties of fitting doctrine into the framework of reality. This did not necessarily make him less intransigent, but, if you will excuse a stray Irish bull, it did make his intransigence more flexible. I mean by this that during the prolonged pause for reflection and regrouping in the mid-1920s he moved further away from the extreme

Seán O'Sullivan, R.H.A., with his portrait of de Valera painted in 1940.

Jerome Connor with his bust of de Valera in 1938.

than created the protectionist policy—fundamental to Sinn Féin from its earliest days—behind which new industries were to be laboriously fashioned, and the ultimate outcome of the quarrel with Britain was the establishment of a state of affairs—enshrined in the External Relations Act óf 1936 and in the Constitution of 1937—which in effect realised the objective of external association as de Valera had set it out 15 years earlier in Document No. 2.

Nor were other strands in his policy in any sense revolutionary. Whether one looks at the Constitution, at the attempts to foster the Irish language, at the emphasis on "anti-partition", or, negatively, at the comparative neglect of social welfare, the general impression one receives is the same. What de Valera had in mind, it would seem, was a small God-fearing country, Gaelic but united, predominantly rural in composition though self-sufficing in other ways, and virtuously turning its back on the sinful seductions of the modern world. Unity apart, he probably came nearest to his ideal during the Second World War, when his skill and tenacity in preserving neutrality gave him an overwhelming personal ascendancy south of the border, while the physical circumstances of the time combined to turn the country into something not very far removed from its idiosyncratic Utopia.

Failures and achievements

In so long a period of power there were bound to be both failures and achievements. As for the latter, posterity may ultimately decide that the chief of these were the virtual destruction of the Treaty settlement, with its immense consequences for the Commonwealth as well as for Ireland; the return of the Treaty ports in 1938; the Constitution of 1937, which, despite the criticisms it has attracted in the very different situation of recent years, provided a degree of stability which was sorely needed; the avoidance of a spoils system in the civil service, the police and the armed forces; the maintenance of internal security in a violent time; the beginnings of the new industrialism; the reconciliation of the Protestant minority to the changed condition of things in the 26 Counties; and, finally, the maintenance of a neutrality in the Second World War which was for de Valera

For almost six decades de Valera was at the centre of the Irish stage.

a principle so deeply embedded that he would not abandon it even when tempted by Britain with the possible ending of partition.

This list, though by no means complete, has to be balanced by a list of failures which, although also not complete, is still considerable. In the possibly unfair light of hindsight we would probably now place first the fact that the anti-partition propaganda seems never to have been matched by constructive proposals about how to deal with the North, while the crudity of the propaganda itself revealed a remarkable insensitivity to the fears and needs of Northern Protestants. It would probably be true to say also that the policy of the Gaelic revival—though its inadequate attainment must have been one of de Valera's deepest disappointments—may well have increased the dislike of Northern Unionists for what they were being offered. This dislike, as we are now told so frequently, can only have been intensified by the new Constitution, objectionable to them both because of its claim to the whole territory of Ireland and also by reason of the Catholic ethos it so obviously reflected.

Nearer home also there were shortcomings. Despite the drive for self-sufficiency, the country remained economically backward and the standard of living for large sections of the population sadly deficient. The fact that so many of de Valera's fellow-countrymen registered their

Once he claimed that he had only to look into his heart to know what the Irish people wanted.

opinion of the prospect he held out to them by emigrating in appallingly large numbers tells its own melancholy tale.

Fleeting resemblance

Not all of this, naturally, can be laid at the door of one man. Both the achievements and the limitations belonged to a government, not an individual, yet that individual was so dominant that historians will surely be justified in describing the 1930s and 1940s as the age of de Valera. It was his age not merely because he stamped his own rigid and powerful personality upon it, but also because, like many great men, he symbolised rather than moulded the period which he bestrode. Nowadays we look back to that period with strangely mixed feelings— envious of its simplicities, vexed by the inheritance it has bequeathed us. But it is salutary to reflect that perhaps the Ireland of

that already remote time really did, if only fleetingly, resemble the image which de Valera held in his mind's eye.

It was poor, it was backward, it was narrow, it was Puritan, but it was also, in a strange way, innocent and yearning, with a dignity of aspiration which mitigated some of its manifest deficiencies.

It may even be that future generations will see in Eamon de Valera, who all his life cared and thought deeply about the democratic process, one of Emerson's "representative men", whose stature derives not just from his own ability but from his harmony with the mood and temper of the people he leads. When he claimed on a famous occasion that he had only to look into his heart to know what the Irish people wanted he may, at least sometimes, have been nearer the truth than cynical observers have ever been prepared to admit.

The seeds of division

by Terence de Vere White

When a statesman becomes a world figure, and especially after he dies, it requires an effort of imagination—or a knowledge of local politics that most people are without—even to consider that he is not necessarily loved by all in his native land. If he has, or had, opponents and critics, to an outsider these will be seen as envious or churlish or both. History has set its seal on this man, and it is a vain exercise to go against it. Even at home, when a great man outlives his contemporaries, he is seen as a rock that stands when the tide recedes, and there is a certain shrillness and ill-nature about any attempt to suggest that it was not always so.

When Eamon de Valera died, aged 92, there were some who thought that the Taoiseach, Liam Cosgrave, was insufficiently fulsome in his tribute to the dead statesman. In his own time de Valera had always been economical with tribute when those outside his political fold departed the scene. These occasions tempt journalists to invite comment from people known to have had ancient quarrels with the deceased, and measured sympathy—such as de Valera was wont to give—is attributed to coldness of heart. Integrity is involved; de Valera, it will be remembered, was one of the few of Winston Churchill's great contemporaries to stay away from his funeral.

Liam Cosgrave is the son of the man who, in the post-Treaty years, was de Valera's chief antagonist. The reality behind the existence of the two principal political parties in the Republic is the Civil War. So sharp and deep was this division that it kept vital social issues out of Irish politics for more than half a century.

Mixed reception

I had once a long private interview with Eamon de Valera. Why he had agreed to meet puzzled me at first because he was guarded and cold in his manner. A well-meaning friend had set up the interview with the hope that it might lead to a book of some kind. De Valera at the outset— this was about 25 years ago—made it plain that he entertained no collaboratory ideas. He referred me to Dorothy Macardle's history *The Irish Republic* if I wanted to know his views although, he added, since then they had not always seen eye-to-eye.

As there seemed to be no point in my staying, and my presence was obviously giving him no pleasure and was wasting his time, I suggested that I should go. But he would not agree to that. Having made it clear that he would not collaborate in a book he still, it appeared, had something he wished to say. He began to talk, and hardly drew breath for over an hour. My interventions were few, and were put down at once. At the close he became quite genial and said that he would always be glad to look over whatever I wrote if I submitted it to him. And on that we parted.

I recorded my impressions of that interview in *A Fretful Midge* when my recollection was still vivid. Looking back at it now, after de Valera's death, I put a different interpretation on his behaviour.

At the time I had recently written a book about Kevin O'Higgins. I attributed the rather chilly nature of de Valera's welcome to the fact that he had only discovered this after he had made an appointment to see me. I had had an almost identical experience before I wrote the O'Higgins book. W. T. Cosgrave had extended a cordial invitation to me to dine with him and discuss his former colleague. On the day we were to have met he rang up to cancel the invitation, saying that he was on his way in to Dublin to call on me. It appeared that he had been priming himself before we met by glancing through the index of a book I had written about Isaac Butt, and found two references to himself. These were inartistically introduced according to my present taste in these matters and, in this instance, fatal to my relations with Cosgrave. In one of the offending passages I remarked how much kinder the English were to someone who kicked them about as de Valera did than to Cosgrave, who stuck to his bargains.

When Cosgrave appeared, he denounced me for saying this and denied the truth of the assertion. He spoke very loudly for several minutes, and then withdrew. I stayed silent, then saw him to the door. It banged behind him.

Getting record straight

Certainly when the name of O'Higgins came up, I thought I noticed steel in de Valera's manner, but I may have imagined it. In the light of the experience of four historians whom de Valera summoned in the last decade of his life for a long briefing session, my interpretation of the incident now is that he could not let the opportunity pass to put the record straight. He wanted to discuss the matter that weighed most on his conscience, and that was his conduct in relation to the Treaty. I thought at the time that what was uppermost in his mind was to justify his attitude after the Treaty had been signed. Here, if I may repeat myself, is what he said to me. I wrote it down at the time.

"You will be asking me if there is anything I regret. I only regret one thing and I often reproach myself on account of it. I was wrong not to order the arrest of the delegation when they returned from London having signed the Treaty."

I lacked the courage to ask de Valera how plenipotentiaries could be arrested for exercising the powers voted them by parliament and who could have arrested them. He did not wait for questions and continued as one who had been brooding long and now wanted to have his say out. *"I think a great deal of the trouble was caused by the I.R.B. When I was a commandant in the Volunteers before the Rising, I discovered that men under me were getting information which was being withheld from me. I asked the reason and discovered it was because they were in the I.R.B. I did not want to join it but I said to myself I must not be at this disadvantage, so I joined in order to have the right to get the information that men under my command were getting. The I.R.B. had a lot to do with the trouble over the Treaty."*

I formed the view then, and it is a subjective one—there is no evidence to support it—that de Valera's anger when he heard a treaty had been signed was because he had counted on an impasse and planned to go over on his own and make the final settlement with Lloyd George.

If this had a place even at the back of his mind it will never be disclosed. What I now see de

William T. Cosgrave . . . after a drawing by Seán O'Sullivan.

Valera's bringing up the subject did reveal is the topic, above all others, that must have preyed incessantly on his mind: his refusal to lead the delegation. He has given his reasons; he gave them at the time. Griffith agreed to go: *"I am willing to be a scapegoat."*

"I have signed my political death-warrant", Birkenhead said when he put his signature to the document. *"I have signed my death warrant"*, Collins replied. So he had.

Political acumen

De Valera was a consummate politician. He may have distracted his mind with mathematics; but politics was his element and he revelled in it. He must have known as well as Griffith, as well as Collins, that there would have to be some compromise and that whoever made it would be handed on a plate to the doctrinaire Republicans and that class which comes into its own at times of revolution and prefers anarchy to the limited opportunities of ordered existence. Not that I accuse de Valera of having planned the destruction of his two most powerful colleagues, or of having wished to avoid the personal risks attendant on making a settlement, rather do I see him as having been over subtle. The Dáil at his own insistence had given its five agents plenipotentiary powers. They went free and unfettered to make the best settlement they could. De Valera in public insisted upon that. But in private he gave them written instructions to refer the terms back to Dublin before they put their signature to a treaty.

Had they done this, it was a reasonable calculation that the pragmatic Lloyd George would have made some further concession to finish the business. Even if it was comparatively trivial—a change in a phrase—if de Valera could have told the country that he had improved on the best terms the plenipotentiaries had been able to obtain, he would not only have stolen the show, he would have rescued them from the responsibility and its consequences.

They did what they did. Two of them died in consequence (it is not far-fetched to attribute Griffith's fatal illness to strain). Two others repudiated their signatures and long survived. By signing they ruined de Valera's plan (if it was his plan). But even if he had no such plan, then his remorse should have been greater, and, yet, mulling it over in his mind, he must have persuaded himself that all would have been well if only they had held out, refused to be browbeaten by Lloyd George, and referred back to Dublin for final instructions.

That Griffith and Collins decided to ignore de Valera and their critics in his Cabinet seems the obvious explanation for their final act of

Kevin O'Higgins and his wife at the Dublin Horse Show, a year before his assassination in the summer of 1927. O'Higgins was Minister for Justice in the Cumann na nGaedhael Government.

101

independent judgement, but it does not explain why two of the delegation, who were most reluctant to sign, and who afterwards repudiated their signatures, did not suggest a telephone call to Dublin. But neither of them ever claimed to have. They were all at the end of their tether, and Lloyd George was a man with diabolical powers of persuasion.

Civil War broke out in June, 1922. Recalcitrant Volunteers had seized points of vantage; in Dublin these included the Four Courts and the Kildare Street Club. It was when with cannon, borrowed from the British, fire was opened on the Four Courts that the Civil War may be said to have begun.

Foresaw the outcome

From this calamity, the most awful that can befall a country, derived the two principal parties in the present Dáil. The seeds from which they sprung were planted then. It was not a direct confrontation between Griffith and Collins on the one hand and de Valera on the other. He had led the campaign in the country before the election; and the aphorisms which are credited to him (he was not of an epigrammatic turn) derive from those hysterical months. *"The people have never a right to do wrong"*, is one of them, and its variant, *"the majority had no right to do wrong"*. How was "right" to be defined or ascertained in a particular situation? He gave the clue when he said: *"I had only to examine my own heart and it told me straight off what the Irish people wanted"*. He foresaw what was to come. *"If they accepted the Treaty, and if the Volunteers of the future tried to complete the work the Volunteers of the last four years had been attempting, they would have to complete it, not over the bodies of foreign soldiers, but over the dead bodies of their own countrymen. They would have to wade through Irish blood, through the blood of the soldiers of the Irish Government, and through, perhaps, the blood of some of the members of the Irish Government in order to get Irish freedom."*

De Valera complained that his words were misinterpreted by his opponents. They were uttered at a time that did not lend itself to minute analysis by malefactors. They had a tocsin sound. He had said, *"If you don't fight today, you will have to fight tomorrow."* When

Michael Collins . . . a bronze cast by the sculptor, Seamus Murphy, after a study in wood by his father-in-law, Joseph Higgins.

the fighting broke out de Valera described himself as a humble follower of Rory O'Connor, who had styled himself Commandant-General of the Volunteers. During the months that followed, de Valera wandered, sometimes it seemed aimlessly, round the country; but when the fighting drew towards a close he emerged as the political leader of the Irregulars, as the force opposing the Treaty was called at the time.

What was the battle about? When an honorary degree was conferred on the late Seán T. O'Kelly, a former President, by Dublin University, the public orator on that occasion used a form of words which suggested that the Civil

*Back in power . . .
his first broadcast
as leader of the new
government after
victory in the 1932
election.*

War was fought on the issue of Partition. Nobody at the time corrected this. In fact the difference between the disputants was the form of oath which was to be written into the Constitution. Partition was mentioned by only one speaker (Seán MacEntee) in the Treaty debate. In a private session of the Dáil de Valera produced what was called "Document No. 2". It was a treaty of which he felt he could approve. When it was not accepted, he withdrew and tried to suppress it—an attempt that failed. In fact it was almost an exact replica of the document in dispute. The references to the excluded six counties was the same, so were the provisions by which the British continued to occupy the ports. The oath to the king was gone.

This had been the subject of protracted discussions before the Treaty was signed. De Valera did not refuse to accept any oath. In private he had agreed to a formula that ran as follows: "I do swear to bear true faith and allegiance to the Constitution of Ireland, and the Treaty of Association of Ireland with the British Commonwealth of Nations, and to recognise the king of Great Britain as Head of the Associated States."

Rather than excite civil war, which he had seen in Spain, the Duke of Wellington withdrew his opposition to Catholic Emancipation in 1829; would that example had been followed over the matter of a form of words.

Taking of the oath

After the Civil War, de Valera appeared as the leader of the Opposition to the Government in power. For five years he kept out of the Dáil, then, after the election of 1927, when the newly constituted Fianna Fáil Party won 44 seats (only three less than Cosgrave's), he announced that he had obtained a legal opinion from three members of the Irish Bar that there was no authority in anyone to exclude any member from the House before the chairman was elected. Armed with this, de Valera led his followers into Leinster House; but the clerk of the Dáil insisted that they must first take the oath before they could enter the Chamber: de Valera then pledged himself, in a public statement, never to take an oath to a foreign king. Shortly after this Kevin O'Higgins was murdered, and the Government then introduced legislation which made it mandatory for any candidate for election to give an undertaking before going forward to take his seat if elected. De Valera then took the oath over which there had been a Civil War. Here is his own explanation:

"Believing that 'I swear' would mean an oath, I said, in my opinion, it was an oath. My view was that it was an oath. But the Deputies opposite had said quite differently. They said that it was not, that it was a mere formality— they used the words long before I used them— and had no binding signficance whatever, that anyone could take it, and that it meant nothing. I asked myself whether in a crisis like that I would be justified in staying outside if it were, in fact, true that this thing was a mere formality. I could only find out in one way. In order that people's attention should not be attracted to it, instead of taking the oath—as they would have done, if they dared to stand over it as a thing the Irish people would stand for—publicly, as in other Parliaments, they hid it away in a back room, hid it away out of sight, so that the public could not know what it was. I said that at least we were entitled to find out.

"We published a declaration and here is the original document, signed by every member, in which we stated our attitude. The attitude was in fact this: the majority party of that time held that this was no oath at all; we are going to put it to the test. In order that our coming in here might not be misrepresented we made a public declaration as to what our intentions were. When we came to take this so-called oath I presented this document to the officer in charge and told him that that was our attitude—there were witnesses present for every word—that this was our attitude; that we were not prepared to take an oath. I have here the original document written in pencil, and in Irish, of the statement I made to the officer who was supposed to administer the oath. I said, 'I am not prepared to take an oath. I am not going to take an oath. I am prepared to put my name down in this book in order to get permission to go into the Dáil, but it has no other significance.' There was a Testament on the table and in order that

there could be no misunderstanding I went and I took the Testament and put it over and said, 'You must remember I am taking no oath'."

Within five years de Valera was to assume office; and he ·remained in power—with two short breaks when a coalition was made against him—until 1959, when he retired from active politics and was elected to the Presidency.

In the years that followed the Treaty W. T. Cosgrave led the Government that had as its only considerable opponent, de Valera, outside the Dáil.

Prisoner of the past

It was an absurd position. Cosgrave was trying to drive de Valera into the Dáil, and the latter was not less anxious to lead a Fianna Fáil Government, but he was a prisoner of his past. The manner in which he extricated himself led naturally to adverse comment. If the oath could be treated like this, why had it ever been necessary to go to war about it? Civil War meant that a river of blood divided the country. It could not be forded as the bitterest political controversy can. Time—a long time—has to pass before the wounds heal.

From this remove, de Valera can be seen as more forward-looking than his opponents. Under the influence of the elder Erskine Childers he proposed the idea of a Republic within the Commonwealth which at the time was regarded as a cranky proposal, unworthy of discussion. This was the formula Nehru used to settle India's position after independence, shortly after this country abruptly left the Commonwealth. But de Valera had no part in that.

No politician has ever clung so persistently to his course as did de Valera. He was adept at keeping the ship afloat and moving forward against contrary winds. His consummate political skill was employed with greater effect and to the satisfaction of his people when he avoided the pressures of Britain, Germany, and the United States during the last World War, and kept Ireland out of the conflict. He was then a cooler and more experienced man than the opponent of Griffith in the Dáil. At that time he exhibited a somewhat disingenuous manner of reconciling apparent opposites. As, for example; when he began the Dáil discussion of the Treaty in Irish which translated reads, *"My Irish is not as good as I should like it to be. I am better able*

Father and son . . . William T. Cosgrave, who in the post-Treaty years was de Valera's chief antagonist, and Liam Cosgrave, the Taoiseach.

to express my thoughts in English, and so I think I had better speak wholly in English." He continued in English: *"Some of the members do not know Irish, I think, and consequently what I shall say will be in English."*

There is a mischievous temptation which is never resisted, to ask a man's opponents to comment at his death. De Valera on these occasions was always guarded. In like manner the present Taoiseach refused to be trapped into insincerity when approached after de Valera died. The son of the man who bore the burden of government in the first years of the State, when he and his colleagues were threatened with death by de Valera's supporters, it was impossible for the Taoiseach, as his father's son, ever to forget that tragic chapter of history or de Valera's share of responsibility for what took place.

That Eamon de Valera did not himself take the lead in the Civil War has never relieved him of full responsibility for it in the eyes of his opponents. The late Richard Mulcahy expressed this to me when he said: *"He could have prevented it by sending a post card to an evening paper."* That was his estimate of de Valera's influence in the country at the time. Merely to mention these matters is to re-open the door to an almost endless debate. It is not proposed to conduct it here.

Historians in the future may decide de Valera was on the right course throughout and put the whole responsibility for the Civil War on the signatories of the Treaty and the Provisional Government which implemented it. Or they may not. What has been written here is probably enough to explain to anyone not acquainted with what happened in de Valera's earlier career why there are doubts in some minds about his claim to the unqualified gratitude of his people.

Document No. 2

The following is the Counter-proposal drafted by Eamon de Valera as an Amendment to the motion for Approval of the Articles of Agreement. He intended to move the Amendment on January 4, 1922.

"That inasmuch as the "Articles of Agreement for a treaty between Great Britain and Ireland", signed in London on December 6, 1921, do not reconcile Irish National aspirations and the Association of Ireland with the Community of Nations known as the British Commonwealth, and cannot be the basis of an enduring peace between the Irish and the British peoples, Dáil Eireann, in the name of the Sovereign Irish Nation, makes to the Government of Great Britain, to the Government of the other States of the British Commonwealth, and to the peoples of Great Britain and of these several States, the following Proposal for a Treaty of Amity and Association which, Dáil Eireann is convinced, could be entered into by the Irish people with the sincerity of goodwill":

Proposed Treaty of Association between Ireland and the British Commonwealth

In order to bring to an end the long and ruinous conflict between Great Britain and Ireland by a sure and lasting peace honourable to both nations, it is agreed

Status of Ireland

1. That the legislative, executive, and judicial authority of Ireland shall be derived solely from the people of Ireland.

Terms of Association

2. That, for purposes of common concern, Ireland shall be associated with the States of the British Commonwealth, viz:—The Kingdom of Great Britain, the Dominion of Canada, the Commonwealth of Australia, the Dominion of New Zealand, and the Union of South Africa.

3. That when acting as an associate the rights, status, and privileges of Ireland shall be in no respect less than those enjoyed by any of the component States of the British Commonwealth.

4. That the matters of "common concern" shall include Defence, Peace and War, Political Treaties, and all matters now treated as of common concern, amongst the States of the British Commonwealth, and that in these matters there shall be between Ireland and the States of the British Commonwealth "such concerted action founded on consultation as the several Governments may determine".

5. That in virtue of this association of Ireland with the States of the British Commonwealth, citizens of Ireland in any of these States shall not be subject to any disabilities which a citizen of one of the component States of the British Commonwealth would not be subject to, and reciprocally for citizens of these States in Ireland.

6. That, for purposes of the Association, Ireland shall recognise His Britannic Majesty as head of the Association.

Defence

7. That, so far as her resources permit, Ireland shall provide for her own defence by sea, land and air, and shall repel by force any attempt by a foreign Power to violate the integrity of her soil and territorial waters, or to use them for any purpose hostile to Great Britain and the other associated States.

8. That for five years, pending the establishment of Irish coastal defence forces, or for such other period as the Governments of the two countries may later agree upon, facilities for the coastal defence of Ireland shall be given to the British Government as follows:

(a) In time of peace such harbour and other facilities as are indicated in the Annex hereto, or such other facilities as may from time to time be agreed upon between the British Government and the Government of Ireland;

(b) In time of war such harbour and other naval facilities as the British Government may reasonably require for the purposes of such defence as aforesaid.

9. That within five years from the date of exchange of ratifications of this Treaty a Conference between the British and Irish

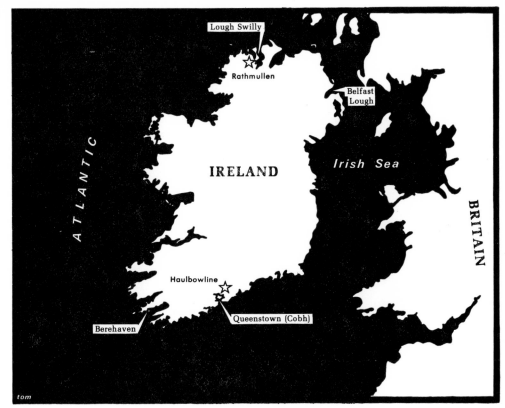

The British naval bases in Ireland in 1922, referred to in the annex to de Valera's counter-proposal to the Treaty terms.

Governments shall be held in order to hand over the coastal defence of Ireland to the Irish Government, unless some other arrangement for naval defence be agreed by both Governments to be desirable in the common interest of Ireland, Great Britain, and the other Associated States.

10. That, in order to co-operate in furthering the principle of international limitation of armaments, the Government of Ireland shall not:

(a) Build submarines unless by agreement with Great Britain and the other States of the Commonwealth;

(b) Maintain a military defence force, the establishments whereof exceed in size such proportion of the military establishments maintained in Great Britain as that which the population of Ireland bears to the population of Great Britain.

Miscellaneous

11. That the Governments of Great Britain and of Ireland shall make a convention for the regulation of civil communication by air.

12. That the ports of Great Britain and of Ireland shall be freely open to the ships of each country on payment of the customary port and other dues.

13. That Ireland shall assume liability for such share of the present public debt of Great Britain and Ireland, and of payment of war pensions as existing at this date as may be fair and equitable, having regard to any just claims on the part of Ireland by way of set-off or counter-claim, the amount of such sums being determined in default of agreement, by the arbitration of one or more independent persons, being citizens of Ireland or of the British Commonwealth.

14. That the Government of Ireland agrees

The return of the "Treaty ports" . . . British troops quitting Spike Island in Cork harbour in 1938.

to pay compensation on terms not less favourable than those proposed by the British Government of Ireland Act of 1920 to that Government's judges, officials, members of Police Forces and other Public Servants who are discharged by the Government of Ireland, or who retire in consequence of the change of government elected in pursuance hereof:

Provided that this agreement shall not apply to members of the Auxiliary Police Force, or to persons recruited in Great Britain for the Royal Irish Constabulary during the two years next preceding the date hereof. The British Government will assume responsibility for such compensation or pensions as may be payable to any of these excepted persons.

15. That neither the Parliament of Ireland nor any subordinate Legislature in Ireland shall make any law so as either directly or indirectly to endow any religion or prohibit or restrict the free exercise thereof, or give any preference or impose any disability on account of religious belief or religious status, or affect prejudicially the right of any child to attend a school receiving public money without attending a religious instruction at the school, or make any discrimination as respects State aid between schools under the management of different religious denominations or divert from any religious denomination or any educational institution any of its property except for public utility purposes and on payment of compensation.

Transitional

16. That by way of transitional arrangement for the Administration of Ireland during the interval which must elapse between the date hereof and the setting up of a Parliament and Government of Ireland in accordance herewith, the members elected for constituencies in Ireland since the passing of the British Government of Ireland Act in 1920 shall, at a meeting summoned for the purpose, elect a transitional Government to which the British Government and Dáil Eireann shall transfer the authority, powers, and machinery requisite for the discharge of its duties, provided that every member

of such transition Government shall have signified in writing his or her acceptance of this instrument. But this arrangement shall not continue in force beyond the expiration of twelve months from the date hereof.

Ratification
17. That this instrument shall be submitted for ratification forthwith by His Britannic Majesty's Government to the Parliament at Westminster, and by the Cabinet of Dáil Eireann to a meeting of the members elected for the constituencies in Ireland set forth in the British Government of Ireland Act, 1920, and when ratifications have been exchanged shall take immediate effect.

Annex
1. The following are the specific facilities referred to in Article 8 (a):

Dockyard port at Berehaven
(a) British Admiralty property and rights to be retained as at the date hereof. Harbour defences to remain in charge of British care and maintenance parties.

Queenstown
(b) Harbour defences to remain in charge of British care and maintenance parties. Certain mooring buoys to be retained for use of His Britannic Majesty's ships.

Belfast Lough
(c) Harbour defences to remain in charge of British care and maintenance parties.

Lough Swilly
(d) Harbour defences to remain in charge of British care and maintenance parties.

Aviation
(d) Facilities in the neighbourhood of the above Ports for coastal defence by air.

Oil Fuel Storage
(f) Haulbowline and Rathmullen: To be offered for sale to commercial companies under guarantee that purchasers shall maintain a certain minimum stock for British Admiralty purposes.

2. A Convention covering a period of five years shall be made between the British and Irish Government to give effect to the following conditions:

(a) That submarine cables shall not be landed or wireless stations for communications with places outside Ireland be established except by agreement with the British Government; that the existing cable landing rights and wireless concessions shall not be withdrawn except by agreement with the British Government; and that the British Government shall be entitled to land additional submarine cables or establish additional wireless stations for communication with places outside Ireland.

(b) That lighthouses, buoys, beacons, and any navigational marks or navigational aids shall be maintained by the Government of Ireland as at the date hereof and shall not be removed or added to except by agreement with the British Government.

(c) That war signal stations shall be closed down and left in charge of care and maintenance parties, the Government of Ireland being offered the option of taking them over and working them for commercial purposes subject to British Admiralty inspection and guaranteeing the upkeep of existing telegraphic communication therewith.

(The following addendum concerning N.E. Ulster was to be proposed as a separate resolution by the President.)

Addendum: North East Ulster
Resolved: That, whilst refusing to admit the right of any part of Ireland to be excluded from the supreme authority of the Parliament of Ireland, or that the relations between the Parliament of Ireland and any subordinate Legislature in Ireland can be a matter for treaty with a Government outside Ireland, nevertheless, in sincere regard for internal peace, and in order to make manifest our desire not to bring force or coercion to bear upon any substantial part of the Province of Ulster, whose inhabitants may now be unwilling to accept the national authority, we are prepared to grant to that portion of Ulster which is defined as Northern Ireland in the British Government of Ireland Act of 1920, privileges and safeguards not less substantial than those provided for in the Articles of Agreement for a Treaty between Great Britain and Ireland signed in London on December 6, 1921.

Neutrality defended

The reply of de Valera to the attack by Winston Churchill on Ireland's neutrality in the Second World War is still remembered by many people, both at home and abroad. "The whole of Ireland stood up and cheered de Valera", said Owen Sheehy Skeffington, writing 17 years after the event. Two of de Valera's phrases stand out: "It is indeed hard for the strong to be just to the weak," and "By resisting the temptation to invade Ireland, Churchill, instead of adding another chapter to the bloodstained record of relations between England and this country, has advanced the cause of international morality."

Probably only the Irish leader and the British Premier knew how close invasion had been and, indeed, if Churchill had not been restrained on at least one occasion, it might have taken place. There was first the conscription crisis, then the Dunkirk disaster and finally the prelude to the opening of the second front in June, 1944. The threats had been combined with promises of a united Ireland, in 1940 and again in 1943–44, and promises of arms and supplies. But de Valera remained steadfast and resisted every move to commit the Irish nation to war.

In the course of a victory speech, broadcast on May 13th, 1945, the British Prime Minister, Mr. Churchill, said:

Owing to the action of Mr. de Valera, so much at variance with the temper and instinct of thousands of southern Irishmen, who hastened to the battle-front to prove their ancient valour, the approaches which the southern Irish ports and airfields could so easily have guarded were closed by the hostile aircraft and U-boats.

This was indeed a deadly moment in our life, and if it had not been for the loyalty and friendship of Northern Ireland, we should have been forced to come to close quarters with Mr. de Valera, or perish for ever from the Earth.

However, with a restraint and poise to which, I venture to say, history will find few parallels, His Majesty's Government never laid a violent hand upon them, though at times it would have been quite easy and quite natural, and we left the de Valera Government to frolic with the German and later with the Japanese representatives to their heart's content.

When I think of these days I think also of other episodes and personalities, I think of Lieutenant-Commander Esmond, V.C.; Lance-Corporal Keneally, V.C.; Captain Fegen, V.C., and other Irish heroes that I could easily recite, and all bitterness by Britain for the Irish race dies in my heart.

I can only pray that, in years which I shall not see, the shame will be forgotten and the glories will endure, and that the peoples of the British Isles and of the British Commonwealth of Nations will walk together in mutual comprehension and forgiveness.

THE BROADCAST
Three days later Mr. de Valera broadcast to the nation on Radio Eireann. The text of his address was:

Go mbeannaí Dia dhíbh, a chairde Gael. Is libhse, a Ghaelgeóirí, is ceart dom an chéad fhocal a rá. Tá an cogadh san Eoraip caite. Ba é deonú Dé, as méid A mhórthrócaire, sinn a shábháil ar an troid agus ar an dóirteadh fola agus sinn a chaomhnadh ar an bhfulang atá ag céasadh furmhór tíortha na hEorpa le cúig bhliana anuas.

Níor tháinigeamar slán ó gach cruatan ar ndóigh—is fada fairsing a theigheas droch-iarsmaí cogaidh. Ach, nuair a chuimhnimíd ar na tíortha agus na daoine go léir mór-thimpeall orainn, is ceart dúinn ár mbuíochas croí a ghabháil go dílis dúthrachtach le Dia na Glóire as ucht sinn a chaomhadh in am an gháibh.

An uair ba mhó a bhí an chontúirt ag bagairt orainn, d'iarras oraibh-se, a Ghaela, seasamh sa mbearna bhaoil chun an náisiún ag chaomhnadh. Bhí a fhios agam go mbeadh fonn ar na

De Valera broadcasting from Radio Eireann on May 16, 1945, his famous reply to Churchill's criticism of Ireland's neutrality during the Second World War.

Gaeilgeoirí, na daoine is fearr a thuigeas céard is brí agus beatha don náisiúntacht, bheith ar tosach imeasc na bhfear a bheadh ina sciath cosanta ar thír na hEireann.

Nior chlis sibh orm, a Ghaela. Rinne sibh bhur gcion féin den obair—an obair a rinne, faoi dheonú Dé, sinn a thabhairt slán le cúig bliana anuas.

Caithfidh mé anois tionntó ar an mBéarla. Tá rudaí áirithe ba mhian liom a rá agus a chaithfear a rá sa teanga sin.

The long and fearful war which has devastated Europe has at last, mercifully, come to an end. And my first object in speaking to you tonight must be to try to express in words the gratitude to Almighty God with which all our hearts are full. I am assured that we shall be able to arrange for a day of national thanksgiving on which we may publicly express due gratitude to God for His immense mercy in our regard.

To the people of all the nations which have been directly involved in the war our thoughts go out in sympathy on their deliverance from the daily terrors in which they lived, and in sorrow that they must still endure the inevitable suffering of the aftermath. We have been spared what so many nations have had to undergo, and there lies upon us, accordingly, a duty, within our limited power, to assist in succouring those who have been less fortunate than we have been.

I have here before me the pencilled notes from which I broadcast to you on September 3, 1939. I had so many other things to do on that day that I could not find time to piece them together into a connected statement. From these notes I see that I said that noting the march of events your Government had decided its policy the previous spring, and had announced its decision to the world.

The aim of our policy, I said, would be to keep

our people out of the war. I reminded you of what I had said in the Dáil, that in our circumstances, with our history and our experience after the last war and with a part of our country still unjustly severed from us, no other policy was possible.

I did not have to go into any details then as to what precisely were the circumstances to which I referred, nor had I to go into detail as to what were our experiences after the last war, nor had I to point out what a vital factor in our situation was the partition of our country. I had merely to refer to them and I felt sure you would understand. Similarly, I do not think it necessary to dwell upon them tonight.

Unified support

I pointed out then that the policy adopted had the backing of practically the entire Dáil and the entire community, irrespective of any personal views which citizens held on the merits of the cause which occasioned the conflict.

That national policy then announced was thus supported by a unity rare to find amongst democratic peoples, a unity tested through two free general elections in 1943 and 1944, a unity which happily survived with us to the end. All political parties and all sections are entitled to their share of credit for what that unity has achieved. It has been a triumph of national understanding and good sense.

There were times when we stood in the gravest danger. But we have been preserved from the calamity of invasion, and such privations as we have suffered in our economic life have been by comparison very slight indeed.

The dire economic consequences which might have been anticipated were prevented by the united efforts of our people, by the co-operation of the public representatives of all parties, by hard work, by careful organisation, and by being enabled to obtain supplies from other countries, particularly Britain, the United States and Canada.

I know you all feel with me the deep debt of gratitude we owe to all those who, at heavy personal sacrifice, joined the Army, including the Marine Service, and the various auxiliary defence organisations and helped to guard us against the most serious of all the dangers that threatened.

The officers, non-commissioned officers, and

Inspecting air-raid shelters at the College of Surgeons in Dublin in 1940 with Frank Aiken.

men of the Regular Army already in service at the beginning of the war formed, with the Reserve and the Volunteer Force, a well-trained nucleus round which it was possible, in an incredibly short time, to build up an efficient fighting force.

Many tens of thousands of young men responded to the appeals of the Government, and of the leaders of all the political parties in the Defence Conference, to join the Army. Without regard to their own personal interests, these young men left their employment or the studies which they had been pursuing in preparation for professional careers.

Auxiliary services

Many thousands of others joined the Local Defence Force and the Maritime Inscription, and made it possible for the Army to feel confident that our best-equipped striking force would be capably assisted by large bodies of well-trained men through the country.

The Local Security Force, the different branches of the Air Raid Precautions Services, the Irish Red Cross Society, the St. John Ambulance Brigade, the Knights of Malta also made themselves available to provide services without which it would not have been possible for us to face, with any degree of confidence, the dangers of the military situation outside.

To all of these, to the many other voluntary bodies who helped in the national effort and to the men of our merchant marine, who faced all the perils of the ocean to bring us essential supplies, the nation is profoundly thankful.

We have survived the ordeal, but I am sure you all realise that the end of the war in Europe does not mean an immediate, or even an early, ending of the period of emergency.

The world is still in a most unsettled state and what may still happen no one can prophesy. Many difficulties concerning supplies of essential goods which the war created will still continue and there can be no relaxation of the regulations relating to the distribution or use of the commodities that have had to be kept under control.

It is, indeed, probable that for a time supplies of some important goods will be scarcer than ever. A great war is still in progress in the Far East, the requirements of which will be a first demand on the productive resources and the shipping of the countries from which, in times of peace, we were accustomed to import great quantities of goods. There is, moreover, a grave shortage of food in many European countries and a danger of famine in many parts of the Continent next winter.

We cannot, therefore, safely look to other countries to make good the deficiencies in our own production. Not merely will international transport difficulties remain acute, but other peoples will have prior call on such supplies as may be available.

Rationing and other forms of control of the distribution and use of goods will have to be maintained so long as the scarcity continues, and can be terminated only when normal supplies are again freely available.

It is of the utmost importance, therefore, that there should be no relaxation whatever in the effort to produce all the food possible from our own soil. There is every indication that the world food situation will be very serious, not merely this year but for a considerable time to come, and that within the next few years we will have to rely on our own efforts to produce the bulk of the food required to maintain the life and the health of our people.

Visiting the troops during the Emergency, with General Hugo Mac Neill and Oscar Traynor, Minister for Defence.

Members of the Council of State assembled on a platform at the Bank of Ireland, College Green, Dublin, for de Valera's public address on national emergency measures after the declaration of the Second World War in September 1939. The party included W. T. Cosgrave, William Norton, James Dillon, Seán MacEntee, Gerald Boland, John A. Costello, Oscar Traynor, Frank Aiken, Frank Fahy (Ceann Comhairle) and Alfie Byrne, Lord Mayor of Dublin.

We must, indeed, not only reduce to a minimum our dependence on imported foodstuffs but, by increasing production, endeavour to make substantial quantities available also for peoples who have been less fortunate than ourselves.

Aid for Europe

So far as this year is concerned, the intention to provide food from our own resources to help in warding off starvation in European countries can be put into effect only by reducing the supplies available for our own consumption. This may, in fact, involve not merely the reduction for a time of the present rations of some commodities, but the extension of rationing to other commodities not now subject to control.

As to the future, there is no likelihood of any material change in the requirements in regard to compulsory tillage for the year 1946 as compared with those in operation in 1945.

The difficulties which we have experienced during the past years in regard to fuel will also remain. There are no prospects whatever of any early resumption of coal imports on anything approaching a normal scale and our domestic fuel needs and the requirements of industry must, in this coming winter, be met by turf.

The Government desire to restore normal trading conditions as early as possible, and no control or regulations will be kept in force for one day longer than is strictly necessary.

The controls established by the Government to prevent inflation must also be maintained for the time being. It will be remembered that it was after the end of hostilities in 1918, and because of the too early removal of the wartime checks on expenditure, that inflationary forces got out of control.

The economic disorganisation which caused so much hardship and distress in later years had its origin at that time. I know that these restrictions are irksome but in the national interest it is necessary for me to ask you to accept and bear them patiently until the danger is past. Again you may be certain that the Government will remove them as soon as it is found safe to do so.

Certain newspapers have been very persistent in looking for my answer to Mr. Churchill's recent broadcast. I know the kind of answer I am expected to make. I know the answer that first springs to the lips of every man of Irish blood who heard or read that speech, no matter in what circumstances or in what part of the world he found himself.

I know the reply I would have given a quarter of a century ago. But I have deliberately decided that that is not the reply I shall make to-night. I shall strive not to be guilty of adding any fuel to the flames of hatred and passion which, if continued to be fed, promise to burn up whatever is left by the war of decent human feeling in Europe.

Allowances can be made for Mr. Churchill's statement, however unworthy, in the first flush of his victory. No such excuse could be found for me in this quieter atmosphere. There are however, some things which it is my duty to say, some things which it is essential to say. I shall try to say them as dispassionately as I can.

Code of necessity

Mr. Churchill makes it clear that, in certain circumstances, he would have violated our neutrality and that he would justify his action by Britain's necessity. It seems strange to me that Mr. Churchill does not see that this, if accepted, would mean that Britain's necessity would become a moral code and that when this necessity became sufficiently great, other people's rights were not to count.

It is quite true that other great Powers believe in this same code—in their own regard—and have behaved in accordance with it. That is precisely why we have the disastrous succession

De Valera favoured sandals during the summer months, even at official functions.

of wars—World War No. 1 and World War No. 2—and shall it be World War No. 3?

Surely Mr. Churchill must see that if his contention be admitted in our regard a like justification can be framed for similar acts of aggression elsewhere and no small nation adjoining a great Power could ever hope to be permitted to go its own way in peace.

It is, indeed, fortunate that Britain's necessity did not reach the point when Mr. Churchill would have acted. All credit to him that he successfully resisted the temptation which, I have no doubt, many times assailed him in his difficulties and to which I freely admit many leaders might have easily succumbed. It is, indeed, hard for the strong to be just to the weak but acting justly always has its rewards.

By resisting his temptation in this instance, Mr. Churchill, instead of adding another horrid chapter to the already bloodstained record of the relations between England and this country, has advanced the cause of international morality an important step—one of the most important, indeed, that can be taken on the road to the establishment of any sure basis for peace.

As far as the people of these two islands are concerned, it may, perhaps, mark a fresh beginning towards the realisation of that mutual comprehension to which Mr. Churchill has referred and for which he has prayed and for which, I hope, he will not merely pray but work also, as did his predecessor who will yet, I believe, find the honoured place in British history which is due to him, as certainly he will find it in any fair record of the relations between Britain and ourselves.

That Mr. Churchill should be irritated when our neutrality stood in the way of what he thought he vitally needed, I understand, but that he or any thinking person in Britain or elsewhere should fail to see the reason for our neutrality I find it hard to conceive.

Hypothetical invasion

I would like to put a hypothetical question—it is a question I have put to many Englishmen since the last war. Suppose Germany had won the war, had invaded and occupied England, and that after a long lapse of time and many bitter struggles she was finally brought to acquiesce in admitting England's right to freedom, and let England go, but not the whole of England, all but, let us say, the six southern counties.

These six southern counties, those, let us suppose, commanding the entrance to the narrow seas, Germany had singled out and insisted on holding herself with a view to weakening England as a whole, and maintaining the securing of her own communications through the Straits of Dover.

Let us suppose, further, that after all this had happened, Germany was engaged in a great war in which she could show that she was on the side of the freedom of a number of small nations, would Mr. Churchill as an Englishman who believed that his own nation had as good a right to freedom as any other, not freedom for a part merely, but freedom for the whole—would he, whilst Germany still maintained the partition of his country and occupied six counties of it, would he lead this partitioned England to join with Germany in a crusade? I do not think Mr. Churchill would.

Would he think the people of partitioned England an object of shame if they stood neutral in such circumstances? I do not think Mr. Churchill would.

Mr. Churchill is proud of Britain's stand alone, after France had fallen and before America entered the war.

Could he not find in his heart the generosity to acknowledge that there is a small nation that stood alone not for one year or two, but for several hundred years against aggression: that endured spoliations, famines, massacres in endless succession; that was clubbed many times into insensibility, but that each time on returning to consciousness took up the fight anew; a small nation that could never be got to accept defeat and has never surrendered her soul?

Mr. Churchill is justly proud of his nation's perseverance against heavy odds. But we in this island are still prouder of our people's perseverance for freedom through all the centuries. We of our time have played our part in that perseverance, and we have pledged ourselves to the dead generations who have preserved intact for us this glorious heritage, that we too will strive to be faithful to the end, and pass on this tradition unblemished.

Many a time in the past there appeared little hope except that hope to which Mr. Churchill referred, that by standing fast a time would come when, to quote his own words, "the tyrant would make some ghastly mistake which would alter the whole balance of the struggle."

A vision

I sincerely trust, however, that it is not thus our ultimate unity and freedom will be achieved, though as a younger man I confess I prayed even for that, and indeed at times saw no other.

In latter years, I have had a vision of a nobler and better ending, better for both our people and for the future of mankind. For that I have now been long working. I regret that it is not to this nobler purpose that Mr. Churchill is lending his hand rather than, by the abuse of a people who have done him no wrong, trying to find in a crisis like the present excuse for continuing the injustice of the mutilation of our country.

I sincerely hope that Mr. Churchill has not deliberately chosen the latter course but, if he has, however regretfully we may say it, we can only say, be it so.

Meanwhile, even as a partitioned small nation, we shall go on and strive to play our part in the world, continuing unswervingly to work for the cause of true freedom and for peace and understanding between all nations.

As a community which has been mercifully

Greeted by Churchill at 10 Downing Street in 1953. Later de Valera said Churchill "went out of his way to be courteous. After lunch . . . I spoke first of a possible reunification of the country. To this he replied that they could never put out of the United Kingdom the people of the Six Counties so long as the majority wished to remain with them. There were also political factors which no Conservative would ignore."

spared from all the major sufferings, as well as from the blinding hates and rancours engendered by the present war, we shall endeavour to render thanks to God by playing a Christian part in helping, so far as a small nation can, to bind up some of the gaping wounds of suffering humanity.

Agus anois, caithfidh mé slán a fhágáil agaibh. Nuair a bhíos ag caint libh i dtús an choghaidh, chuireas an tír agus a muintir faoi choimirce Dé agus a Mháthar Muire, agus isé mo ghuidhe anocht: Go raibh an choimrí chumhachtach chéanna oraibh san aimsir atá romhainn!

117

A obair mhór ar son na Gaeilge

le Tomás de Bhaldraithe

B'fhánach an obair í féachaint le tuairisc chruinn a thabhairt i gcúpla céad focal ar a ndearna de Valera ar son na Gaeilge ón uair fadó a mbíodh sé ag múineadh sa scoil Samhraidh i dTamhain na Gaillimhe anuas go dtí an glaoch mífhoigh-neach fóin a tháinig le gairid uaidh ag iarraidh foilsiú an fhoclóra nua Gaeilge a bhrostú. Is fada fós go mbeifear in ann breith chóir a thabh-airt ar thoradh an chúraim sin a rinne sé den teanga ar feadh a shaoil, ainneoin a mbíodh de chúraimí cráite cruógacha eile i gcónaí air.

Cé go mbíodh riar éigin Gaeilge, ar a laghad leaganacha is focail, agus Béarla an-Ghaelach le cloisteáil aige le linn a óige i mBrú Rí, b'éigean dó an teanga a fhoghlaim ó bhonn. D'fhág sin tuiscint ar leith aige do dhá ghné dí, sa chéad ait, do shaibhreas dofhoghlamtha Ghaeilge bheo na Gaeltachta, agus sa dara háit, don ghortghlanadh is don eagrú nár mhór a dhéanamh ar an saibhreas uaibhreach ain-srianta sin le go bhféadfaí buneolas uirthi a theagasc, agus í a chur ag obair mar mheán scríofa cumarsáide sa saol nua. Chuir sé scéim ar siúl le saibhreas stór focal a bhailiú ar fud na Gaeltachta—scéim a bhfuair cuid di poiblíocht mhór de bharr shaothar cruthaíoch duine de na bailitheoirí—Seán An Chóta as Corca Dhuibhne. Níor tugadh poiblíocht ar bith do ghnéithe eile den scéim sin, mar shampla, gur iarr de Valera féin ar Mháirtín Ó Cadhain, tar éis dósan teacht as an gcampa géibhinn, dul i mbun bailithe i gConamara—rud a rinne an Cadhnach.

Ní miste beart eile a rinne de Valera a lua—bunú Scoil an Léinn Cheiltigh san Institiúid Ardléinn. Ní airsean a bhí an locht má ba mhó an cúram a rinne lucht na scoile sin den seantanga ná den Ghaeilge bheo—chuir sé cúram na Gaeilge beo go cruinn soiléir san acht bunaithe. Ní airsean ach oiread atá an milleán nár éirigh le lucht na scoile sin ceann de na chéad chúr-aimí a leag sé féin orthu a chur i gcrích—litriú na teanga a ghiorrú is a chaighdeánú. Níor loic sé féin ón iarracht. Mar is eol go maith, chuir sé an cúram ansin ar Rannóg de chuid an Taoisigh, agus lean sé leis ag brostú lucht na rannóige sin go dtí gur thugadar an saothar chun críche. Ba

é féin freisin ba chúis leis an bhFoclóir Béarla-Gaeilge a thionscailt. Ba mhinic le linn na hoibre go mb'éigean dó na húdaráis a bhí ag plé leis a mhioncheistiú is a dheifriú chun saothair.

Taobh amuigh dá thuiscint den teanga mar chuid bhunúsach de dhlúth is d'inneach shaoith-iúlachta na tíre, bhí spéis mhór aige i bhfocail is i dteangacha. Ní hannamh, tar éis an chláir raidió sin *Fadhbanna Gaeilge* a ghlaodh sé orm ag iarraidh tuilleadh eolais, nó ag inseacht cé na leaganacha a bhí cloiste aige féin ina óige—nó ag múscailt ceisteanna eile.

Is ceap milleáin coitianta an fear polaitíochta. Ba mhinic breithiúnas éagórach á thabhairt air mar chainteoir Gaeilge. Is fíor go mbaineadh an róchúram a dhéanadh sé den mhionchruinneas den líofacht—go háirithe ar ndóigh agus é ag dul in aois. Is cuimhneach liom féin, ag comór-adh fhilí Charraig na bhFear sna seascadaí, an óráid bhreá líofa a thug sé as a bhéal don slua mór Gaeilgeoirí a bhí bailithe ann. Ní hionadh sin ar ndóigh ó fhear a thosaigh óráid togh-cháin uair i gCo. an Chláir le sliocht fada as *Cúirt an Mheán Oíche*—dán a bhí de ghlan-mheabhair aige ó thús deireadh, a deirtear. Is eol dúinn, blianta fada ina dhiaidh sin go raibh *An Chúirt* ar théip aige agus í á haithris ag Seán Ó Ceallaigh, iartheachta Dála, Gaeilgeoir dúchais as an gClár.

Má mheath an Ghaeilge i gCo. an Chláir—meath a thosaigh i bhfad sular rugadh de Valera—ní airsean is cóir an milleán a bhualadh. Dhéanadh sé a dhícheall le glúin óg an chontae a spreagadh len í a chleachtadh. Uaireanta ní labharadh sé ach í ag cruinnithe den pháirtí. D'admhaigh an Dr. Ó hIrghile gur chuir sé iallach air líofacht cheart a bhaint amach inti, sula ligfí chun cinn é.

Ní féidir de Valera agus gluaiseacht na Gaeilge a scaradh ó chéile. Má tá glúin daoine anois ann atá in ann litríocht nua a shaothrú, agus leas nádúrtha éifeachtach a bhaint as an teanga i gcúrsaí oideachais, riaracháin is cumarsáide, ní féidir a shéanadh nach faoi anáil de Valera is a dhearcaidh faoin nGaeilge a oileadh iad.

De Valera, de Gaulle agus Dia

le Seán Ó Ríordáin

An té a bhíonn amuigh fuarann a chuid nuachta. Mar sin féin ní féidir gan trácht ar Dev dá dhéanaí sa ló é. Dia ab ea Dev. Ní féidir é mheas mar dhuine bhí sé chomh fada san ina dhia. Cén aithne phearsanta atá againn air i gcomórtas leis an aithne phearsanta atá againn ar Ó Cadhain de bharr a chuid scríbhneoireachta súd? An raibh Dev ann in aon chor ar an slí sin? An raibh aon saol aige ach le linn dó bheith ar taispeáint? Chaith sé cuid mhór dá shaol amhlaidh. Ón uair go bhfuil Dev marbh mhothófá go mb'fhéidir go bhfuil deire le déithe—go bhfuil clapsholas na ndéithe tagaithe. Tá amhras agam air. Ní foláir nó tá glú nua déithe ag fás.

Tá Mao agus Franco fós ann. Sórt dé is ea Paisley agus bhí Bernadette ag foghlaim chun a bheith ina bandia nuair a chuaigh sí as amharc. Tá súil agam go bhfillfidh sí. Chomh fada lem eolas b'é Picasso dia deireanach na n-ealaíontóirí. Tá roinnt bheag déithe fágtha san litríocht —Sartre, Beckett, Solzhenitsyn. Déithe ab ea Joyce agus Ó Cadhain. Níl aon dia polaitíochta fágtha sa Phoblacht. Daoine is ea Jack, Cosgrave *et hoc omne genus*. Níorbh aon dia Lemass. Déithe ab ea Collins agus Kennedy. Féachtar ar Chríost mar dhuine, mar bhall de I.R.A. Iosrael, sa leabhar, *The Jesus Scroll*, le Donovan Joyce— leabhar ina ndeintear iarracht ar an gCríostaíocht a bhréagnú ó sháil rinn. Tá an leabhar so suimiúil ar mhórán slithe ach go mór mór toisc a chosúla atá sé le haigne na ndaoine anso in Éirinn fé láthair—stairithe, polaiteoirí, etc.—a labhrann i gcoinnibh an ruda ar a dtugtar creideamh, bíodh an creideamh san polaitiúil nó sprideálta. Dí-dhiaú Chríost atá ar siúl ag Donovan Joyce. Tá dí-dhiaú Dev ar siúl le fada. Is mór leo a thoirt sa tsolas.

Nuair a cailleadh Dev bhí a shoiscéal agus a shampla dulta in aigne na ndaoine. Bhí ré déanta de Dev. Bhí an ré sin agus ar lean í chomh seanbhunaithe, chomh mór ina cuid dínn, nár aithníomair í. Cheapamair gurbh í an t-aer í nó an saol. (Bhí daoine áirithe a fhan laistigh de dhóirse iata uaithi ach bhlais gach aoinne í.)

De Valera le Seán Ó hEochaidh (An Fear Mór) le linn cuairt a thug sé ar Choláiste Rinne, Co. Port Láirge, Lúnasa, 1951.

Cheap an t-aos óg agus aosa ná raibh chomh hóg gurbh í an *status quo* nó an aigne oifigiúil í agus d'ionsaíodar í agus táid á hionsaí agus de réir dealraimh á treascairt mura bhfuil sí treascartha acu. Ar an dtaobh eile den scéal b'fhéidir nach á treascairt atáid ach ag tógaint uirthi. Má thug fear riamh pobal chun a chló féin thug de

119

De Valera i gColáiste na bProinsiasach i mBaile Ghormáin, Co. na Mí, ar ócáid oscailte ionaid teangeolaíochta, Márta, 1965.

Valera. Más fíor conus a aithneofaí é thairis an bpobal san? Ar deire ní raibh sé le haithint mar b'é an pobal é. Bhí sé dulta i bhfolach in aigne na ndaoine. Mar sin féin bhí sé de chuma air le tamall fada go raibh sé beo tar éis a bháis féin, gur mhair sé le ré nua—an ré iar-Dev d'fheiscint.

Tá stairithe áirithe ag díspeagadh de Valera fé láthair agus ag móradh Dhónaill Uí Chonaill. Téann an dá rud le chéile de réir dealraimh. Colceathar do Churchill ab ea Ó Conaill agus colceathar do de Gaulle ab ea de Valera. "Bligeárdaithe" móra ab ea Churchill agus Ó Conaill. B'fhearr leo feall ná fealsúnacht; b'fhearr leo camastaíl ná creideamh: b'fhearr leo bheith daonna ná bheith ceartchreidmheach. Bhí samhail den bhFrainc in aigne de Gaulle agus samhail d'Éirinn in aigne de Valera. Ba mhó a suim araon sa tsamhail ná ins na daoine —ar mhaithe leis na daoine. De réir prionsabail a oibríodh de Valera agus de Gaulle; de réir mar oirfeadh don ócáid a oibríodh an bheirt eile. Bhí an dá shórt aigne riamh ann agus iad i gcónaí in earraid lena chéile. Ní foláir nó caithfidh siad araon a bheith ann chun smacht a choimeád ar a chéile agus chun an daonnacht a iomlánú.

B'é de Valera an duine ba mhó draíocht dá bhfeaca riamh. Chonac don gcéad uair é ag labhairt i gCorcaigh i 1933. Ní dhearmhadfad go deo é. Mhothaíos go rabhas i láthair na staire. Ní mise amháin a bhí goilliúnach—más é sin an focal ceart. Bhí na mílte fé dhraíocht. Ní dhearmhadfad an aghaidh chneasgheal, an cló iasachta a bhí ag teacht lena shloinne Spáinneach, na súile stairiúla ar lasadh, na spéaclaí, an béal, an tsrón fhada, a aoirde. Níorbh fhéidir é shamhlú gan spéaclaí. Ba mhó ná duine é dar leat. Is cuid d'aigne an uile dhuine geall leis sa Phoblacht an aghaidh sin le breis is 50 bliain agus ní hí an telefís a leath a phictiúir. Tá aithne agam ar dhuine go raibh sé de nós aige sceitseanna a dhéanamh de Dev ón gcéad lá go bhfeaca sé é breis is 30 bliain ó shin agus d'aosaíodh a chuid sceitseanna de réir mar a aosaíodh aghaidh de Valera. Ní chuirfeadh aghaidh de Valera cor di ná téadh i bhfeidhm orainn go léir. Ach cad a imeoidh ar na sceitseanna anois? An stopfaidh siad nó an n-aosóidh siad a thuille?

Fear creidimh ab ea de Valera ar nós Dhónail Uí Chorcora nó Mháirtín Uí Chadhain. Níl aon uair dár labhras le hÓ Corcora nó le hÓ Cadhain ná gur neartaigh an teagmháil mé. Neartaíodh sé mé de Valera a chlos nuair a bhí sé in aoirde a láin. Neartú creidimh ab ea an neartú so uaireannta ach uaireannta eile níorbh ea ach neartú ort féin. Ba mhó de dhuine tú toisc bheith ina láthair. Nuair a chonacaís de Valera chonacaís duine a bhí dar leat níos láidre ná cinniúint an duine. Má fhéadfadh duine amháin bheith amhlaidh cad ina thaobh ná féadfása?

Ach cad a chreid sé? Chreid sé gur náisiún ar leith Éire agus nach cuid de Shasana í. Ba ghile leis an creideamh so ná a shaol féin. Chreid sé chomh maith ná féadfadh an náisiún maireachtaint gan an Ghaeilge mar theanga náisiúnta— ní mar fhochultúr. Chreid sé na nithe seo go huile is go hiomlán—go láidir. Fear láidir ina bhreithiúntas ab ea é. Bhí an sórt céanna nirt ag an gCadhnach agus ag an gCorcorach. Bhíodar triúr ionraic, éirimiúil agus chuir san lena n-údarás. Le linn dom bheith ina láthair nuair a bhíodar in aoirde a láin—agus bhí an Cadhnach in aoirde a láin go lá a bháis—níor tuigeadh domsa ach go háirithe gurbh aon teoiriciúlacht a gcuid creidimh ach léam fírinneach ar an saol. Chreideadar triúr sa Chríostaíocht dar ndóigh.

Bhíodh de Valera beagán leamh le linn dó teanga liotúirgeach an náisiúnachais a labhairt, ach is é a bhí spéisiúil le linn dó bheith ag imirt fichille le Lloyd George nó le Churchill nó leis na Léinteacha Gorma. Taibhsí cuid mhó dá chuid óráidí dátaithe anois ach tá a chuid beartaíochta, a chuid fichille, chomh friseáilte inniu agus bhí an chéad lá. Polaiteoir cruthaitheach ab ea é den chéad scoth. Is mar sin a chuir sé é féin in iúl. Sin é maraon lena chreideamh a dhein mór é. Tá an mhilseacht chéanna ina státaireacht súd agus tá i bprós Uí Chadhain. De réir mar thagann na páipéirí stáit chun solais chímíd cad é an cluiche aoibhinn a imir sé le linn Chogadh Hitler nuair a bhí na Déithe Móra, Churchill, Hitler, Roosevelt, ag drannadh leis ó gach taobh agus Stalin aca mar chárta cúil. Tá cáiliíocht éigin piocaithe, blasta, urnua, ag baint lena chuid fichille. Cén bhaint a bhí ag creideamh leis an imirt seo nuair dob é Dev a bhí féin neamhspleách ar chreideamh? Is cosúil gurb é an creideamh a thug an misneach dó chun aghaidh chomh dána a thabhairt ar a chuid namhad agus chun cluiche chomh fuarchúiseach a imirt.

Tá sé curtha ina leith ná raibh ann ach taoiseach Caitliceach agus nár chuir sé Protastúnaigh an Tuaiscirt san áireamh—má ba Mhaois dúinne é nárbh aon Mhaois dóibh san é. B'fhéidir go bhfuil cuid den bhfírinne ansan. Tar éis is ea a tuigtear gach beart agus is fuirist sprioc chomh mór le Dev a bhualadh. Níor thriall sé riamh orthu an plámás atá sa bhfaisean anois—plámás ná fuil éirithe rómhaith leis, is cosúil. Ar a laighead bhí fáilte aige rompu agus dhein sé iarracht ar náisiúntacht dhúchais a athbhunú anso a thabhairt rogha níos ciallmhaire agus dídean níos cluthaire dóibh ná an rogha agus an dídean maide atá á dtairiscint dóibh anois.

Dúirt Breandán Feiritéar ar Radio na Gaeltachta le déanaí go bhfuil Dev chomh préamhaithe san mbéaloideas i gCorca Dhuibhne le hAristotle nó Naomh Pádraig nó Brian Bóraimhe. Dúirt Jimmy Mhártain ar an gclár céanna gurbh iad Dev agus Brian Bóraimhe an bheirt ba mhó dá raibh riamh in Éirinn agus cé nár mhaith leis Brian a chur síos go mb'fhearr Dev. "Níor rug aoinne barra ach é seo," dúirt sé. "É seo is mó a thug relief dos na daoine bochta. Chonac ar an gCill é ag caitheamh ceaiste. Bhí ana-urchar ceaiste aige."

Eamon and Sinéad on the golden anniversary of their wedding, January 8, 1960.

The only family photograph of Eamon and Sinéad and all their children: standing (from left)—Ruairí, Vivion, Eamon, Brian; sitting (from left)—Máirín, the parents, Emer; kneeling—Terry. Brian died shortly after this picture was taken in 1936.

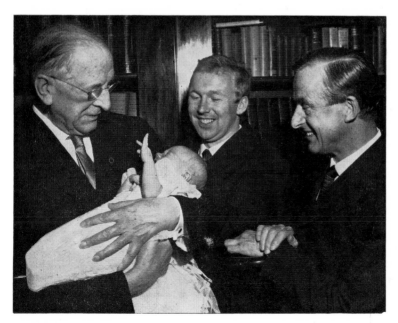

Four generations of de Valeras: Eamon de Valera holding his great grandson, Eamon Annraoi, with the child's father, Eamon de Valera, and his father, Professor Eamonn de Valera.

The family gathering at Áras an Uachtaráin in October, 1962, to celebrate Eamon de Valera's 80th birthday: Eamon (6) and Sinéad (4); Vivion (2) and his children, Ann (20) and Eamon (16); Máirín (8); Eamonn (28) and his wife, Sally (11), and their children, Eamon (26) and Máire (27); Ruairí (30) and his wife, Eithne (10), and their children, Eithne (13), Eamonn (14), and Ruairí (1); Brian Ó Cuív (29) and his wife, Emer (25), and their children, Nora (22), Máire (24), Caithriona (23), Vivion (21), Shan (15), Eamon (17), Brian (18), Ruairí (7) and Eoin (3); Terry (19) and his wife, Phyllis (12), and their children, Síle (9) and Jane (5).

Sinéad de Valera avoided the limelight

by Eileen O'Brien

The first time that de Valera looked old was at the funeral on January 9, 1975, of his wife Sinéad. His carriage was erect as he entered the Pro-Cathedral, but when he took his place inside the tears coursed freely down his cheeks. She died the night before their 65th wedding anniversary.

One of her very last appearances in public was at a Gaelic League meeting to hear a splendid talk on its foundation by the Rev. Tomás O Fiaich. Afterwards tea and biscuits were dispensed. The occasion epitomised the dignity and austerity of her life and her life-long devotion to the Irish language.

Sinéad Ní Fhlannagáin began her career as a teacher of young children in Dorset Street. In the evenings the young and charming teacher taught Irish to grown-ups. Among her students was Eamon de Valera.

There was nothing dry about study in the early days of the Gaelic League. There were Irish-speaking holidays in Tourmakeady, Co. Mayo, the production by the Irish Literary Theatre of Douglas Hyde's "An Pósadh" in which she took part and the performance of "The Tinker and the Fairy", in which she also acted, in George Moore's garden in Ely Place. There was a historical pageant in which the part of fat Raymond le Gros was played by a slender youth, Earnán de Blaghd, who was her student and admirer. He declared later that he would not have done it for anyone else.

After her marriage in 1910 she lived quietly. And, though she had won an Oireachtas gold medal for oratory she seldom took any part in public life. Her family life was disrupted by her husband's spells in jail or travels in America. In 1920 she travelled to America on a false passport to visit him.

Later, as her family began to grow up, she wrote the children's plays and stories which for generations of little boys and girls made learning Irish a joy. She adapted old Irish stories and translated European fairy stories into Irish. She also wrote serious plays for the older children, one for example, about the martyrdom of St. Oliver Plunkett.

Later as her husband became Taoiseach and then President, she entertained kings and queens and presidents and visited Pope John.

She performed only one public function when she went to the Verolme dockyard in Cork to launch the *Irish Rowan* for the Irish Shipping company.

On her 90th birthday many presidential and royal messages arrived.

Her former student Earnán de Blaghd—he did not live long after her—wrote then "Sinéad's interest in the Irish language and her work for it never ceased or slackened. Her manifold encouragements to the young and the plays and reading matter in Irish which she provided for them were a factor of importance in keeping the language movement vital . . . When pantomimes in Irish were put on in the Abbey she never failed to come, generally bringing the President. She thereby not only encouraged young people to come but she boosted the morale of the players who might otherwise have been somewhat depressed by consciousness of work for a minority."

President O Dálaigh said on her death that Ireland had witnessed the passing of "a great and gentle soul".

'This election will always be history'

by Brendan O Cathaoir

Eamon de Valera fought his first parliamentary battle in the East Clare by-election of 1917. The election swung the centre of gravity of Irish politics from the Home Rule party towards the Sinn Féin movement. It marked the emergence of Dev as a national leader, and was the beginning of his association with the constituency which lasted for 42 years.

The vacancy occurred on the death of the sitting M.P., Major Willie Redmond, who was killed in Messines on June 7. Local supporters of the Irish Parliamentary Party selected Patrick Lynch, K.C., to oppose de Valera.

The man who carried the Redmondite banner came from an old Clare family; the other candidate was a stranger. But Dev was the senior surviving officer of the Easter Rising and, by 1917, that was sufficient to ensure election. The only surprise was the extent of his victory: 5,010 votes to 2,035.

De Valera stood for the ideals of the 1916 Proclamation. On the Northern question he said in Killaloe: *"Let Ulster Unionists recognise the Sinn Féin position which has behind it justice and right. It is supported by nine-tenths of the Irish people and if those Unionists do not come in on our side, they will have to go under. Ulster is entitled to justice and she will have it, but she should not be petted and the interests of the majority sacrificed to her. Give Unionists a just and full share of representation, but no more than their just share."*

Lynch's forlorn refrain at the hustings was:
Faithful to the memory of O'Neill,
Faithful to the memory of Sarsfield,
Faithful to the memory of the Irish Brigade,
Willie Redmond has died on the battlefields of France.

My grandfather, a first cousin of Lynch, went canvassing for him in the Burren district. He asked the parish priest of Ballyvaughan for his support. The priest, more in touch with changing times than the family, retorted: "I'll vote for no Crown-prosecuting K.C."

Lynch acted as a straw to test the growing storm of Sinn Féin. The campaign was conducted

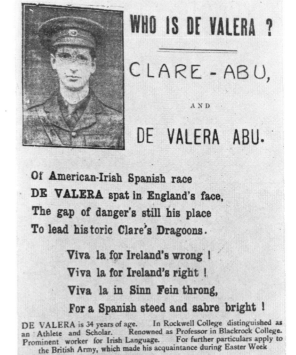

His first election poster, East Clare, 1917.

in a gentlemanly fashion, with both candidates agreeing to avoid mob support.

De Valera, tall and intense and dressed in the banned uniform of the Irish Volunteers, captured the popular imagination. The chant, "Up Dev", re-echoed from the Clare hills into the pages of history. Old men and women, who had never before bothered to vote, went to the polling booths from remote cabins on July 10.

East Clare attracted widespread comment. A Dublin Castle official told a reporter from the *Daily Telegraph* that it was "the most important election that had ever taken place, or ever will take place, in Irish history." For the official, this assessment was not too wide of the mark.

One direct result of de Valera's triumph was that the 1917 Convention, upon the outcome of which John Redmond (Willie's brother) depended for the survival of his party, lost further credibility. Already boycotted by the Republicans, it could no longer accept the parliamentary party's claim to speak for nationalist Ireland.

Dev, returning to thank his followers, said: *"This election will always be history—a monument to the glorious men of Easter Week, who died for us."*

The de Valera Arms

In March, 1966, the Chief Herald of Ireland, Dr. Gerald Slevin, made out a patent of arms to Eamon de Valera, confirming with a personal coat-of-arms, the outline of which is illustrated here.

Based on the ancestral de Valera arms, the shield and crest are typically Spanish in design. The shield is divided into four compartments or quarters, the first and fourth showing a golden rampant lion on a red background, a familiar bearing among families which originated in the Kingdom of Leon. The second and third compartment demonstrate an unusual heraldic precedent, showing four silver crescents on a gold background—it is unusual to place metal on metal in heraldry, the few exceptions include the ancient arms of the Kings of France and the City of Jerusalem.

The shield is surrounded by a red border containing eight small silver saltires—the border is a common emblem in Spain, and is generally associated with the Kingdom of Castile.

The crest of five plumes is peculiarly continental, the Butlers being one of the few other Irish families to have a similar crest. The plumes alternate in the colours red and gold, the primary colours of the shield, and are placed on a wreath of gold and red.

Patrick Comerford

The Rugby man

by Edmund Van Esbeck   Rugby Correspondent of The Irish Times

Winston Churchill was once asked what went into the make-up of a great statesman. "All of them, in my experience, were rounded individuals whose talents extended across many spheres of diverse activity", was his response. One does not know if he numbered Eamon de Valera among those to whom he was referring, though he had had reason to appreciate the depths of de Valera's intellect and skill as statesman and politician.

The life and times of de Valera, scholar, statesman, soldier and politician are etched in the minds of all Irishmen. The lesser known side of his career is that which surrounded his sporting activity. Patronage of the sporting occasions when he achieved such eminent positions as leader of government and subsequently President of Ireland, indicated a catholic taste in the sporting sphere. But he was, above all in the field of sport, a rugby man.

Giving credence to Churchill's assessment of the statesman, there is ample testimony to the abilities in the sporting arena of many politicians. One prime minister of France, for instance, was also a rugby international, another represented his country at lawn tennis.

De Valera never achieved such eminence in his rugby career. And while legend in respect of his playing activity has to a great extent superseded fact, he was nonetheless a player of no mean degree of skill who knew what it was to participate in the turbulent drama of a Munster senior cup campaign.

Initiation at Blackrock

De Valera's formative years were spent in Bruree, Co. Limerick, unlikely rugby territory at that time, but it was not surprising that, when he entered Blackrock College in 1898, he would soon be introduced to the game in what was then and still is one of Ireland's foremost rugby-playing schools. His introduction as a player came during the Christmas vacation of 1898, when he spent the holidays in the college. There is no record of any great prowess on his part during the next four years, all spent in the

college, for when he finished his secondary education he stayed on as a resident in The Castle, while he studied for his university degree.

It is a widely held belief that he was a member of the Blackrock College past pupils' team that won the Leinster Junior Cup in 1899, but this is incorrect. In fact, he was still a college student that year. However, he did play a part in the victory celebrations as one of the students who chaired the captain of the side, Paddy Heffernan, all the way from Lansdowne Road back to the college.

He went to Rockwell College in 1903 and there it was that his career on the rugby field blossomed: he became a player of senior team standard. With such famous men as the internationals Mick and Jack Ryan as teammates, de Valera played many fine games for Rockwell in the Munster senior cup. He was, according to contemporaries, a versatile player, being able to perform with equal facility at full-back, wing or in the centre. The late Dick Magrath, an Irish international, who died only two years ago, told me that he well remembered playing against de Valera and described him as a player of "some consequence" though he could never remember him being in the running for representative honours. *"He was quick and had a very good kick".*

Try disallowed

Perhaps the most famous match in which he played was the semi-final of the Munster Senior Cup in 1905 against Cork Constitution.

The late Mossy Landers, an Irish international full-back and later the distinguished rugby correspondent of the *Cork Examiner*, wrote a graphic description of the background to, and activities in, that match, in a rugby annual produced 40 years ago.

"During the years 1905, '06 and '07, Cork Constitution were invincible. They had built up the ideal team. Constitution won the Munster Cup for the first time in 1905. That year we met Rockwell in the semi-final of the cup in Cork and

De Valera, the rugby player (seated, right). It was at Rockwell College, Co. Tipperary, in 1903, that his interest in the game blossomed; he played in the Munster senior cup and in the semi-final against Cork Constitution and scored a try. He was very disappointed when the try was disallowed because of an earlier infringement.

won. But after an objection the game was ordered to be replayed in Limerick.

"The famous Louis Magee was the referee and four minutes from full time with the scoresheet blank, Magee told us it was extra time if that state of affairs remained. We were awarded a penalty and Jim Musgrave kicked the goal. But the game was by no means over and up came Rockwell and a scrum was formed 10 yards from our line. The Rockwell backs broke away and Magee blew his whistle and pointed to the still unbroken scrum, but in the general din, the Rockwell backs did not hear the whistle.

"One of their centres—a tall player with a fine turn of speed and grim-set features—raced over the line to ground far out. He was very disappointed when he discovered his try disallowed. That centre was Eamon de Valera."

"Many years later", wrote Landers, "Mr. de Valera was reminded of his rugby exploits in Munster and remarked: 'Those were happy days'."

That was probably the last match de Valera played for Rockwell, for he returned to Dublin in October, 1905, after a very brief spell in Liverpool. He took up a teaching appointment in

I am very glad to learn that the centenary of the Irish Rugby Football Union is to be commemorated and that already the story of Irish rugby is being compiled. It is a centenary which will stir the heart and memory of every follower of the game, old and young, player and spectator alike.

The Union has served Ireland well and has through the years given us reason to be proud of our place in this international field. At national level, its organisation has served to promote the athletic values of rugby and the spirit of discipline characteristic of the game.

I wish the Union every success. Bua agus forás go raibh mar thoradh ar a shaothar.

8 Feabhra, 1973.

De Valera's letter to the Irish Rugby Football Union for its centenary in 1974.

Belvedere College and his interest in the game was maintained. He, together with a J. J. Tallon, represented Belvedere College at the annual general meeting of the Leinster Branch at the Gresham Hotel on October 6, 1905.

Centenary greeting

He returned to Blackrock the following year and once again his name is recorded in the minutes of the Leinster Branch as having, with a Mr. Smithwick, been one of two Blackrock College representatives at the annual general meeting of 1906. That his interest in the playing and administrative sides of the game was considerable can be judged from the fact that he was also at the general meeting of 1907, again representing Blackrock College.

In those years, he played regularly for the second XV and, indeed, was captain of the team in 1908–09, when, after he announced his intention to marry, he gave up his active participation.

Events were to follow such a course in his full life from now on, that there was little time for sport of any kind, but he maintained a keen interest in rugby throughout his life. When he heard that the history of the Irish Rugby Football Union was being written to celebrate the centenary of the Irish rugby body, he wrote, while he was still President of Ireland in February 1973, wishing the project and the union every success. He had in his own humble way helped to fashion that history, being one of the thousands who had played the game and obviously loved it.

Return to Bruree and his own people

It was a great day for Bruree when the child who once won a prize for sums in its school returned for his ninetieth birthday celebrations as President of Ireland, on October 8, 1972. Bruree was in a mood to throw its Republican principles to the four winds and crown de Valera king of Ireland.

Heuston Station was carpeted in red when the President and his party boarded the State—formerly royal—train. It gleamed with polished mahogany and burnished brass. There were antimacassars of Carrickmacross lace and a hand basin of Connemara marble. The ghost of plump Edward VII was exorcised by the austere dignity of the President and the youthful charm of the pretty C.I.E. hostess who attended his party.

Austerity yielded to joy at Rathluirc when the President left the train and sniffed his native air. The cavalcade stopped at an ancient site, Cnoc Dotha, which he maintained was second in importance only to Newgrange.

Excitedly he examined this evidence of the history of the district, a history so long that it loses itself in the mist of legend with a fierce fairy woman cutting off the ear of a local king who vexed her. De Valera spoke poignantly of his blindness: *"Bhí mór-bhrón orm nach*

Nostalgic moment . . . seated at his first school desk in Bruree, Co. Limerick, when he visited the locality of his childhood on October 8, 1972.

raibh an radharc agam a bhí agam fadó nuair a b'fhéidir liom an tír ar fad a fheiceáil ón áit sin."

When he arrived at Bruree, the little town was a whirl of musicians, bishops, F.C.A., Old I.R.A. and the entire population. There was a 1916 veteran among them, Mr. Michael Collins. A huge birthday cake with green, white and orange icing had been baked and relics of a little boy had been piously assembled in the new museum in the old school which would be known thenceforward as Aras de Valera: a copy book signed Eddy de Valera, a lock of curling blonde babyish hair.

After a triumphal march, the President addressed his people, his enthusiasm mounting as he recalled macghníomhartha-like cooking a wedding breakfast, winning a case of pencils as a prize for sums or travelling prodigious distances in pursuit of learning. It was not easy: he had to give up school for a long period to mind his infirm grandmother; when the time came for an important examination he was stricken with measles—but with steely determination got there all the same; he was forced to waste valuable time listening to a man named Jack Cotter "who spoke very nice cultured English"; he would rather listen to two journeymen tailors, the Connollys, who were wonderful story-tellers, but his grandmother would not allow him out at night to listen.

But there were compensations. The school was comfortable: *"We paid a shilling at the beginning of each winter. It bought coal which made the school nice and cosy. I never felt cosier —and I do not think I had an overcoat."* There were also conversation lozenges acquired from an old woman named Bridget Carroll and the occasional tomhaisín of snuff.

It was pouring rain, but the hardy 90-year-old did not care. The farmers needed it, he observed. All the boys of the town had climbed upon the platform. Half-way through the speech it started to collapse. Boys and dignitaries were sent flying, but the President kept imperturbably on. As he warmed to his speech the years fell away from him. For de Valera, like Rafferty, his own people were the elixir of youth: *"Dá mbeinnse 'mo sheasamh i gceart lár mo mhuintir, d'imeodh an aois diom is bheinn arís óg . . ."*

Then de Valera led the procession to the school dated 1862 where he was met by the

Mainchin Seoighe, the Bruree historian, showing de Valera the display of mementoes of his career in the school-museum at Bruree during his visit as President on October 8, 1972.

Newcastle West Pipers. His fellow countrymen pressed around him so zealously that his two daughters, Dr. Máirín de Valera and Mrs. Brian O Cuiv, could not get in at all, but were left with others of the principal guests outside in the rain. But everyone remained good-humoured and joy was unconfined.

And, as Mainchin Seoighe, the historian of Bruree, declared, it was the most historic day that Bruree had ever known. *"O ró shé do bheatha abhaile, a Eamoin de Valera."*

132

Childhood home and school are shrines

by Donal Musgrave

The small roadside labourer's cottage where de Valera was reared in Knockmore, Co. Limerick, and the grey stone national school in Bruree, beside the River Maigue, where he once carved the initials "E.D." into a wooden desk have become instant shrines to his memory.

Since his death many hundreds of people have visited the village to see such mementos as his old handwriting exercise books, a jacket and shirt, the roll book, and a mildewed leather school bag in the three-down two-up cottage in the heart of the countryside which profoundly influenced the former President, and where in his own words he spent 'some of the happiest moments of my life."

But apart from the steady stream of visitors the life style of Bruree has been relatively unchanged by his passing.

In a village of 270 people where the politics of every house and the three pubs are known political opposition can run deeper than normal. De Valera's opponents still blame him for the Fianna Fáil Government's refusal in 1953 to build a chocolate crumb factory in Bruree. This, despite letters written by him to local people like his friend, the late Dan Sheahan, a farmer and his closest neighbour at Knockmore, explaining that the Government could not establish the factory because the country already had enough of them and also because there were severe market limitations and export uncertainties at the time.

But in spite of such economic realities his local political opponents will still point to the almost empty shells of two milling industries which once employed over 400 men in his youth and ask: "What did de Valera ever do for Bruree?" Against the anti-Dev arguments the curate, the Rev. Anthony O'Keeffe emphasises that *"irrespective of what some people might say de Valera had a terribly great regard for Bruree. He was always very proud of his origin and whenever he got the chance he came around and inquired about the old people. The last time he was here, three years ago, he travelled back over all the old roads that he walked to school seven miles away in Charleville. And he spoke for nearly an hour, re-living his childhood, recalling who sat beside him in school, and details about his teacher and his early life. He loved the area."*

Father O'Keeffe led a special delegation from Bruree to attend the State funeral. It consisted of Mainchin Seoighe, curator of "Aras de Valera", the museum in the national school, Mr. Patrick Lyons, vice-chairman of the Bruree/Rockhill Development Association, and Mrs. Louis Cregan, the voluntary caretaker of the museum. The people of Bruree sent telegrams to the de Valera family saying they were "proud to claim him as one of their own. Bruree has lost its greatest son."

Mrs. Byrdee Sheahan, an alert, articulate lady in her 80s, who knew Dev for 50 years, and lived in the thatched farmhouse across the road from his cottage home, where he first visited as a child, remembers how "he always called here to see me when he came. I was sad and lonely at his passing because every time we met he talked about little details of past times—about the nice home-made bread he liked to eat, about playing hurling in our top field, and about the old stable where, as he told me, *'I had the one day in my life I mitched from school and I went home hungry out of it'.*"

Mrs. Sheahan remembers too how as President he had spent two hours with her daughter, a nun in an enclosed convent in Dublin, during the funeral of her late husband, because she was unable to attend the funeral.

Unpublished letters

Among the mementos collected by the Sheahan family are two previously unpublished letters, illustrating his interest in the simple things of life, and also his detailed memory about local people and events.

In one written in September '68 he recalled when invited to a farewell party for the Rev. O'Mahony, that *"the name of his grandfather, James O'Mahony, was often on my grandmother's lips when I was a child . . . my grandmother lived in the workman's house on the*

The old schoolhouse at Bruree, Co. Limerick, now serves as a museum, Aras de Valera.

farm. The rood of land attached to the house was later incorporated in the half acre of the labourer's cottage which was given to my grandmother at that time.

"The house where the O'Mahony's lived was the first I visited as a child and I was told that a hole in the settee bed in the kitchen was made by a piece of candle that had been fired from a shot-gun by Bill O'Mahony who was regarded as a 'wild youth'.

"The O'Mahonys were succeeded in the farm by the Mortels. On acquiring the farm the Mortels let it for a year to a dairy man named O'Donovan.

"One evening I saw a bright light at the eastern gable of the house. I ran to my grandmother to tell her to come and look at 'Donovan's lamp'. It was in fact the moon just rising. Whenever, for years afterwards, my grandmother spoke to me of the moon she called it 'Donovan's

lamp' . . . 'Donovan's lamp is lit tonight', she would say.

"Our other near neighbours were the O'Sullivans, the McEnirys, the Lyons, the McCarthys, and the Fitzgeralds had the Drumacommer Post Office, but I must not let myself go on or I would write the history of the whole parish."

In another letter to the Sheahans, thanking them for helping him plant a rowan tree beside the well in the field behind his home, he wrote: "I am delighted that the well of which I have such pleasant memories has been restored. I spent there some of the happiest moments of my life. I suppose there are not so many skylarks about now since the field has been drained and reclaimed. In my time the larks seemed to be there by the hundred.

"It was very good of you to have the rowan tree for me to plant. I hope it will grow."

The tree has grown.

The nation's mourning

As the Tricolour fluttered at half mast over Boland's Mills at lunch-time on Friday, August 29, 1975, Dublin gradually realised that Eamon de Valera was dead. By 1 p.m. special editions of the evening newspapers were on the streets. Normal broadcasting on radio and television was suspended and commemorative programmes carried the news to the ends of the nation. His death had been expected and public reaction was subdued rather than shocked. There were few obvious signs of grief. It just felt strange that after all these years he was suddenly no longer there.

President Cearbhall O Dálaigh and his wife drove from Aras an Uachtaráin to Talbot Lodge in Blackrock, Co. Dublin, where the aged statesman had lived since his retirement, to pay their respects. The President said of his predecessor: "Throughout the world, and, in particular, among peoples striving to be free, his name has been a synonym for the struggle for Irish independence." Tributes and messages of sympathy came from political and Church leaders, from foreign heads-of-state and governments, from old friends and life-long opponents. Lord Brookeborough, son of the former Northern Ireland Premier, said: "His name dominated my early life."

After a day of private mourning by the de Valera family, the nation's final act of public homage to its former Chief began. On Saturday evening, shortly after 7 o'c. a bearer party from military police of the Second Garrison Company (Collins Barracks) brought the coffin to the steps of Talbot Lodge where it was mounted on a gun carriage. Twenty boys of Blackrock College, the former President's old school, and members of the local Fianna Fáil cumann lined up in informal guards of honour as motor-cyclists of the Army's Second Motor Squadron (Cathal Brugha Barracks) escorted the cortege out of the grounds of the convalescent home.

In the fading evening light the Tricolour draping the coffin glowed vividly against the dull suburban concrete. Groups of people gathered at the roadside as the long cortege made steady, quiet progress to St. Stephen's Green, Grafton Street and College Green. Here it halted and the motor-cyclists swung away. The gun carriage was given a platoon escort from the Fifth Infantry Battalion (Collins Barracks). The cortege was also joined by a colour party from the same battalion, a new bearer party of military police and pall-bearers drawn from officers of all the corps of the Eastern Command.

The Army No. 1 Band, at a slow march, led the cortege along Dame Street and up to Dublin Castle. The gun carriage went under the arch and into the Castle yard to the strains of "Wrap the Green Flag Round Me".

Military police bearers, accompanied by officers of the Army, Naval Service and Air Corps, carried the coffin into black-draped St. Patrick's Hall. The de Valera family then filed past the former President's body, clad in the brown and white habit of the Carmelite Order, into which he had been received in Rome in 1951, when he visited the Vatican as Taoiseach. Civic and religious dignitaries followed, then a host of old colleagues, veterans of the War of Independence, a party of nuns from Talbot Lodge and his secretary, Máire Ní Cheallaigh. Outside thousands waited their turn in a queue that stretched the whole length of Castle Street and half-way down Werburgh Street as night fell.

70,000 pay tribute

Throughout Sunday, August 31, people passed the catafalque in silent tribute. At intervals, ambassadors and diplomats from the nations of the world called to pay their respects. The Apostolic Nuncio, the Most Rev. Dr. Gaetano Alibrandi, was followed by the ambassadors of Italy, Austria, Belgium, Britain, Japan, Switzerland, Sweden, Russia, Australia and India, the charges d'affaires of Nigeria, the U.S.A., Canada, Denmark, Spain, France, the Netherlands and West Germany. By mid-afternoon the public queue, in places ten abreast, stretched the whole way round the Castle.

When the lying-in-state ended just after five o'clock on Monday afternoon, more than 70,000

An estimated
70,000 people filed
past the body of
Eamon de Valera
during the lying-
in-state in St.
Patrick's Hall at
Dublin Castle.

people had visited the Castle to say farewell to the nation's father figure.

A few hours later the body was transferred from the Castle to the city's Pro-Cathedral. The cortege passed quickly through hushed and crowded streets. More than 1,000 leading members of the Fianna Fáil Party observed 30 minutes' silence at the General Post Office, where he had so often taken the salute at commemorations of the 1916 Easter Rising. They stood to attention as the remains of the last leader of the Rising passed without a pause. All along O'Connell Street people removed their hats and saluted, or made the sign of the Cross.

At the Pro-Cathedral, old comrades, members of the Old I.R.A., lined the steps and the porch as the Archbishop of Dublin, the Most Rev. Dr. Dermot Ryan, and his four auxiliary bishops received the coffin. Covered by the Tricolour it

was laid on a black catafalque before the main altar. A brief ceremony—all in Irish—ended with a decade of the Rosary and the old Irish hymn "Sancti Venite", said to have been written by St. Secundinus, a disciple of St. Patrick. Military sentries, heads bowed, stood guard at the coffin. Other soldiers carried in wreaths, one of them bearing the message— "With deep respect from the officers and men of Boland's Mill 1916 Garrison". The Pro-Cathedral stayed open till midnight as members of the public crowded in to pay their respects.

From early on Tuesday morning crowds gathered around the Pro-Cathedral and along the funeral route: Dubliners old and young, people from the four provinces up for the day, tourists with cine-cameras jostled for the best positions at the front of the crowd barriers. The obvious excitement was respectfully restrained

Members of the former President's family, led by Major Vivion de Valera, were the first to file past during the lying-in-state in Dublin Castle. The body was clad in the brown and white habit of the Carmelite Order into which Eamon de Valera was received in 1951.

as the diplomatic limousines arrived, but the crowd could not resist a short burst of applause when Princess Grace of Monaco appeared.

Requiem Mass in Irish
The mood of the crowd became reverent as the ceremony, relayed outside by loudspeaker, began. The funeral Mass was celebrated in Irish by de Valera's grandson, the Rev. Shan O Cuiv, who wore the white vestments presented to him by his grandfather on the day of his ordination in 1972.

All the great names of the land were there in the Pro-Cathedral. So too were the old men of the Boland's Mill garrison and the G.P.O. garrsion, proudly wearing their War of Independence medals, on their knees clutching their rosaries. Side by side were Frank Aiken,

de Valera's confidant and friend, and Seán Mac Entee—the two remaining members of the original 1932 Fianna Fáil Cabinet.

The Rt. Rev. Mgr. Tomás O Fiaich, President of Maynooth College, preaching in his rich Ulster Irish, reminded the congregation that the message of the Requiem Mass was one of hope, courage and confidence.

As Donal Foley in *The Irish Times* observed next day, hope and courage were never needed more, with the awful news on that most solemn of days that seven more people had been murdered overnight in the North's continuing bloody conflict.

Mgr. O Fiaich told those present that suffering had been a feature of de Valera's life, but in facing trials he had never been found wanting. De Valera, he said, had always remained a

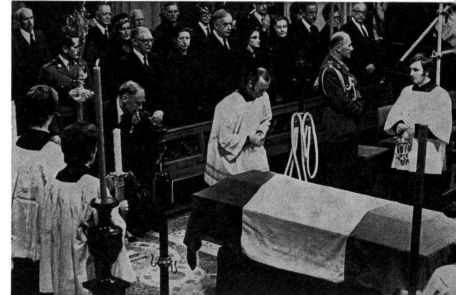

The Rev. Shan Ó Cuiv, grandson of Eamon de Valera, celebrated the Requiem Mass in the Pro-Cathedral.

The Taoiseach, Liam Cosgrave, headed the Government attendance at the Requiem Mass.

In the shadow of the G.P.O., where 59 years earlier the founding of the Irish Republic was proclaimed, members of the Fianna Fáil Parliamentary Party assembled in tribute to their former leader.

Units of the Army and Naval Service escorted the gun-carriage bearing the coffin of de Valera through the centre of Dublin. A silent assembly of more than 100,000 people lined the three-mile funeral route from the Pro-Cathedral to Glasnevin.

simple man, he had never deserted the simple qualities of life that he had learned as a child in Bruree.

As this simple man's coffin was borne with quiet dignity—and the now familiar military precision—to the waiting gun carriage outside the Pro-Cathedral, thousands of people, about half of them small children, had been already waiting for hours at Glasnevin cemetery, tomb of Ireland's freedom fighters, north of the city, to catch a last glimpse of their historic leader.

From de Courcey Square onwards, so massive was the gathering crowd that people overflowed into the heavily barricaded Finglas Road, climbed on high walls and rooftops, or clutched the high ladder up to the press stand. Prams and cameras were everywhere.

Outside the cemetery four officers and 100 men of the Eastern Command rested on arms reversed from 11.00 a.m. The air of formal solemnity was broken briefly when one soldier—and minutes later another—swayed and collapsed. They were immediately removed from the ranks and taken away by ambulance.

In O'Connell Street, there was barely room to move behind the crowd barriers along the entire length of the street as the people waited patiently in the late morning sunshine. A man outside the G.P.O. selling copies of a pamphlet "Dev—His Life and Times" did a brisk trade. Gardai cleared about 50 young people from the top of a wooden hoarding near Eason's which was said to be in danger of breaking under the weight.

The silent assembly

Shortly before mid-day, Garda and Army motor-cycle escorts led the funeral procession into O'Connell Street from Eden Quay. The crowd was stilled. In that magnificent main thoroughfare the only sounds were the murmur of the motor-cycle engines and the slow marching steps of the guard of honour. For the last time de Valera passed the G.P.O. The cortege turned to the right of the Parnell Monument and up Cavendish Row to Parnell Square East.

Northwards from the city-centre, the route was thickly lined with people and every turn and junction gathered its own special crowd. At the Mater Misericordiae Hospital, where de Valera had visited his wife Sinéad during her final illness not many months before, about 30 blue-caped nurses lined the pavement, their white veils fluttering in the breeze. Near Mountjoy Prison, where Mr. de Valera had been held for a while after his reprieve in 1916, a group of Catholic Boy Scouts from Phibsboro and Dominick Street stood to attention as his coffin passed.

Phibsboro was the focus of one of the biggest gatherings in the northern suburbs. The rooftop car park of the shopping centre became a grandstand for hundreds of people and more perched on the roofs of bus shelters and on the cabs of lorries. As the cortege curved through Phibsboro, the bell of St. Peter's tolled solemnly. When the gun carriage came to Finglas Road, the procession slowed to funeral pace for the final march to Glasnevin.

The sun disappeared as Garda motorcyclists approached the cemetery gates at one o'clock. An Air Corps jet flew overhead. As the Army No. 1 Band approached, the first thundering shot of a 21-gun salute caught many unaware, hundreds of startled children burst into tears. The shots continued at one-minute intervals, sending huge flashes and volumes of smoke overhead.

The naval party passed through the double-filed guard of honour, followed by the Army colour party and escort from Eastern Command. The Army band fanned out by the cemetery gates with low strains of "The Dead March in Saul" and the colour party and escort presented arms as the remains of the dead Chief were brought through the gates. Colours were dipped.

The graveside scene

At the grave, the Very Rev. Edward Murphy, parish priest of Louth village, had been waiting from an early hour. Just before the funeral the Rev. Tom Walsh, O.P., chaplain to the Dublin Brigade, Old I.R.A., arrived. Soon after him were the Rev. Pádraig O Fiannachta and the Rev. Micheal Mac Greil, prominent in the Irish language movement, and the Very Rev. Phelim McCabe, chaplain to the Forces. Cardinal Conway, Primate of all Ireland, and Archbishop Cowderoy of Southwark, London (it was in Southwark Cathedral that Terence Mac Swiney, the Lord Mayor of Cork who had died on hunger strike in Brixton in 1920, had lain in state) took their places at the head of the grave, where they were joined by the Archbishop of Dublin, Dr. Ryan. The Papal Nuncio, Dr. Alibrandi, headed

Amid the forest of gravestones at Glasnevin, leaders of State and Church joined the de Valera family as the body of the father of modern Ireland was laid to rest.

the diplomatic corps. Fianna Fáil former Ministers, deputies and senators, followed by members of the Council of State and the present Fine Gael—Labour Coalition Government massed at the graveside.

Meanwhile, the bearer party of military police under Sergeant Charlie Jameson bore the Tricolour-draped coffin through the guard of infantry from Cathal Brugha Barracks under Commandant Tom McGrath.

The de Valera family came to the right of the grave, his sons Vivion, Eamonn, Terry and Ruairí, his daughters Máirín and Emer, his son-in-law and daughters-in-law, a host of grandchildren and one little great-grandchild. Father O Cuiv went with other priests to the foot of the grave. Phyllis, wife of the late President Seán T. O Ceallaigh, Máire Ní Cheallaigh and nuns from Talbot Lodge were with the family. President O Dálaigh and his wife stood opposite the family.

Citizens who had been waiting closed in behind the family. Children perched on the heads of statues or on high Celtic crosses. But the Old I.R.A., who had waited for three hours, failed to get close to the grave as their old leader's coffin was lowered to its final resting place.

A firing party of cadets under Lieutenant Con McNamara fired three volleys over the grave. Trumpeters and drummers from the band of the Western Command sounded the Last Post and Reveille.

The prayers in Irish were led by the Rev Patrick Farnon, de Valera's godson. Fr. O Cuiv and the Rev. Thomas O'Doherty, brother of Mrs. Eamonn de Valera, responded. The Angelus was said by Fr. O Cuiv's uncle, the Very Rev. Shan O Cuiv, parish priest of Blackrock, Co. Dublin.

The names on the headstone over the de Valera grave are those of the former President's

143

son Brian, killed in a riding accident in 1936, of Bríd Bean Vivion de Valera, who died in 1951, of Mr. de Valera's wife Sinéad, who died on the night before their 65th wedding anniversary in January, 1975, and now the name of Eamon de Valera himself.

The grave behind is that of his friend Monsignor Pádraig de Brún, who was president of University College, Galway. Nearby is that of Caitlín Ní Chonaill, for many years de Valera's private secretary, and the grave of Margaret Burke Sheridan, whose singing he admired. Lower down are those of Patrick Ruttledge, James Larkin, Elizabeth O'Farrell who bore the flag of surrender in 1916 and of men of the Connaught Rangers Mutiny in India of 1920.

As the dignitaries of Church and State, the diplomats and the Army moved away, it was the turn of the ordinary people of Ireland to come closer to the grave to pay homage to the man who was Gaelic Leaguer, Volunteer officer, prisoner, president of the Dáil, Taoiseach and President of Ireland.

Tribute in London

In an impressive tribute to Eamon de Valera in Westminster Cathedral, London, on September 25, 1975, diplomats representing 52 nations attended a memorial Requiem Mass at which the principal celebrant was the then Archbishop of Westminster, Cardinal Heenan. He was assisted by the Bishop of Southwark, Dr. Cowderoy, the Bishop of Brentwood, Dr. Casey; and more than 30 priests of the Westminster archdiocese.

The lesson was read in Irish by Dr. Donal O'Sullivan, Ireland's Ambassador in London. The British Government and Opposition were represented at the Mass and the congregation included many M.P.s and peers.

Cardinal Heenan said Mr. de Valera was a statesman of world proportions whose outstanding virtue as a Catholic layman had been his humility. He added: "Like that great Englishman St. Thomas More, Eamon de Valera found time to serve God as well as his country."

Máire Ní Cheallaigh, private secretary to Eamon de Valera, and the Rev. Sister Denis, one of the Sisters of Charity who nursed the former President at Talbot Lodge. Miss Ní Cheallaigh succeeded in 1956 her aunt, Caitlín Ní Chonaill, who had been de Valera's personal secretary for 37 years.